# TORNADO ADV
# PROTECTING BRITAIN'S SKIES

# Tornado ADV
# Protecting
# Britain's Skies

HUGH HARKINS

The Pentland Press
Edinburgh – Cambridge – Durham – USA

First published in 1995 by
The Pentland Press Ltd
1 Hutton Close,
South Church
Bishop Auckland
Durham

ISBN 1-85821-287-1

Typeset by Carnegie Publishing, 18 Maynard St, Preston
Printed and bound in Great Britain by Bookcraft (Bath) Ltd.

# Table of Contents

# Panavia Tornado F2/3 Described

The Panavia Tornado is a tri-national aircraft that was designed to fulfil seven different roles for the air forces of the United Kingdom, Italy, and West Germany, along with the latter country's naval air arm. After the introduction to service another role was allocated to the Tornado, that of defence suppression, with both Italy and Germany procuring the purpose designed Electronic Combat Reconnaissance (ECR) version armed with the US High Speed Anti-Radiation Missile (HARM). Britain meanwhile went to the other road and adopted the ALARM missile for its standard GR MK1s.

Originally the MRCA as it was known was to be built as a NATO war plane, with other countries such as Canada, the Netherlands and Belgium included in the project. After much disagreement all the other countries left except for the three mentioned partners. Canada instead chose the McDonnell Douglas FA18 Hornet designated CF188 in Canadian service while the other two adopted the General Dynamics F16 Fighting Falcon. The workshare for each partner was based on how many aircraft each was to buy, this was 15% and 100 aircraft for Italy, 42.5% each for W. Germany and Britain.

The roles to be undertaken were as follows:

1. Interdiction strike (penetrating to attack targets deep in enemy territory).

2. Counter air attacks (attacks on the enemy's airfields).

3. Battlefield air interdiction.

4. Close air support.

5. Reconnaissance.

6. Point interception.

This last mentioned has not been adopted for any of the users and the British RAF has gone a step further and adopted the Tornado Air Defence Variant to fulfil not the point interception but rather the all-weather day and night interception role. For political reasons, which the author has no desire to go into, the ADV was kept secret even from Britain's Panavia partners for a while, therefore the ADV became an all British aircraft although the various parts were still manufactured in their respective countries. Once out in the open there was much talk of this new fighter, which promised to be amongst the hottest property in the air defence world, being adopted by a number of NATO countries especially the two other partner nations, Italy and then West Germany, neither of which at that time were seriously looking to replace their current fighters, the Lockhead Aeritalia F104S Starfighter and the McDonnell Douglas F4F Phantom respectively.

As it turned out none of the NATO countries showed much interest mainly because of the Tornado's high price tag reported at between £16M and £22M, with most, including the ones mentioned above, adopting cheaper single seat American designs such as the F16 and FA18. No NATO nation other than the US has bought either of the Tornado ADV's American rivals, the Grumman F14 Tomcat or the McDonnell Douglas F15 Eagle for the same high price tag reason. Therefore sceptics who claim that the Tornado ADV was not a successful NATO fighter candidate due to lack of interest in the design couldn't be more wrong. In late 1993 the Tornado F3 as the ADV was known was eventually chosen over the F15 Eagle by Italy as an interim fighter pending the arrival of EF 2000 of which there will be more information in the Export chapter.

The Tornado ADV was adopted for the RAF to fight the predicted air battle over the North Sea; this would have involved large formations of Soviet long range bombers and strike aircraft, some of which would have released cruise missiles at distances of some 300 miles from Britain's shores. To meet this challenge the RAF did not need a small short ranged agile fighter in the F16 Fighting Falcon class, but rather a long range interceptor able to meet the enemy as far from Britain's shores as possible, and shoot him down using Beyond Visual Range missiles such as the excellent BAe Skyflash Semi Active Radar Homing (SARH) missile.

The Tornado FMK3 was ideally suited to this but has, with the disappearing Soviet threat, found itself employed in combat zones of a different nature such as the Gulf and the former Yugoslavia. To compensate for this more traditional air superiority fighter role the aircraft has undergone some improvements, and despite what the ill-informed media seem to think, has emerged a rather surprisingly competent fighter. That is not to say it will not find the going difficult in close combat with some of the current agile fighters such as the F16, FA18 and Mig 29 but the Tornado's superior speed at low level (nothing can catch or get away from a Tornado F3 between the weeds) and better radar detection range do give it some advantages. The Tornado, when fighting to its own rules, is more than a match for anyone.

When speaking to F3 pilots and navigators of 111 Squadron the author was told they were more than confident of meeting any potential opponent, adding that the extra crew member was an advantage over contemporary types such as the USAF F15 Eagle and Russian Su27 Flanker. Indeed the Tornado F3 can even get the better of an F16 in close combat at low altitude.

The main type of fighter opposition likely to be encountered in the traditional air battle mentioned above would have been the extremely capable Su27 Flanker B, which would have operated in the long range fighter escort role, or the long range Mig 31 Foxhound. It is virtually impossible to predict how a fighter-versus-fighter engagement between the F3 and either of the two Russian types would turn out as no aircraft type would be operating alone; both types would be likely to be assisted by other aircraft such as AWACS. For theoretical purposes therefore, let us assume that no AWACS support is available to either side and a pair of F3s and a pair of Foxhounds are approaching each other in a head on engagement. Detection ranges of each type, including the Su27's radar, are given as between 120 and 149 miles; these figures are purely academic as they represent the maximum range; with individual aircraft types having varying Radar Cross Sections (RCS) then different types would be located at different ranges. The RCS of the Tornado and the Su27 are about 3m2 with the Foxhound following at about 5m2, but both the Russian types employ their rather large AAMs on bulky underwing and underfuselage pylons, greatly increasing their RCS, whereas the F3 carries its main armament of four Skyflash missiles semi-recessed under the fuselage to reduce the increase in RCS. On these assumptions therefore, it would be logical to suppose the Tornado would locate its targets first, thus giving it the tactical advantage of setting up a BVR engagement sequence before its opponent. If the fighting becomes close then the Tornado would be more than capable of outmanoeuvreing the cumbersome Mig, although

The first ADV prototype A01 ZA254 banks low over the North Sea. (BAe)

With wings in the 67° position ADV prototype No 2 A02 ZA267 takes on a sleek appearance. (BAe)

against the Su27 at medium and high altitudes it would be at a manoeuvring disadvantage, therefore it would be wise to go down to sea level where the Flanker's advantage is not so obvious. On the other hand the Tornado's close proximity to home and its extra long legs would mean that it would be unlikely to have to break off the fight before either Russian type.

Included in Batch One of Tornado production were three prototype Tornado ADVs. The prototype ADVs have a gantry installed at the base of the fin, which houses a large parachute. In the event of the aircraft entering a spin in which recovery action fails to work the parachute is streamed; this rapidly lowers the nose, reducing the incidence and stopping the spin. Internally the aircraft has an emergency power unit driven by a large hydrazine pump; this provides hydraulic and electrical power to drive the control system in the event of a double engine flame-out during a spin. This has a back up in the form of an electrohydraulic pump which does the same thing. The prototypes carried Skyflash missiles which were painted yellow and had black test crosses for high speed photography of the launch sequence.

To photograph the launch the Tornado had fitted a pair of camera pods in the shape of converted Skyshadow ECM pods, as carried by the Tornado IDS. The windows on the outer face of the pods were blanked off.

The first two ADV prototypes were painted in an attractive black, white and grey colour scheme which made the aircraft highly conspicuous. As with the Skyflash missiles the aircraft were covered in black crosses to assist in analysing high speed photography.

The First ZA254 flew at Warton for the first time on 27 October 1979 with David Eagles at the controls and Roy Kenward in the back seat. Even at this early stage the aircraft was carrying four

The third prototype A03 ZA283 adopted an air defence grey colour scheme similar to that used on the F2/F3. (BAe)

dummy Skyflash missiles. On this first flight that lasted 22 minutes the aircraft exceeded Mach 1 and before a week was out had flown 8½ hours in five flights, and included an air-to-air refuelling and a night landing. These early flights had proved that the ADV had better supersonic acceleration than the IDS variant due to the improved fineness ratio of the fuselage, but the more forward centre of gravity caused the aircraft to demand greater elevator angle at lift-off than that required by the IDS variant.

The second prototype, ZA267, made its maiden flight on 18 July 1980. This was a dual control aircraft and was assigned to weapons development, introducing among other things a main computer and associated cockpit TV displays. The third and last of the prototypes, ZA283, was flown on 18 November 1980. This aircraft had an overall grey colour scheme similar to that adopted by the RAF. This aircraft was to be used for radar development but due to delays with the Foxhunter did not begin trials until June 1981.

The first prototype, ZA254 A01, by the middle of 1980 had flown at an IAS of 800kts (1480km/h) at a height of 2,000ft (610m); this capability would give the ADV a considerable speed margin over most of its potential adversaries as most modern combat aircraft are limited to about 700–750 kts due to structural limitations. This also means that nothing can escape from a Tornado ADV when being pursued at low altitude. The same aircraft demonstrated in early 1982 its ability to fly a CAP of two hours and twenty minutes at a distance of 375nm from base. The aircraft achieved this without aerial refuelling by using 330 gall. (1500ltr) auxiliary fuel tanks as used on the Tornado GR MK1 strike aircraft; this meant that the Tornado F MK3 when it entered service with its more fuel efficient MK104 turbofans and 495 gall (2250ltr) fuel tanks would be capable of much more. To top it off, on its arrival at Warton the aircraft loitered in the airfield's vicinity for 15 minutes before landing with more than 5% fuel remaining.

In the same year A02 carried out various armament trials involving firing Skyflash missiles at M 0.9 up to supersonic speeds. The internal Mouser 27mm cannon was also tested in the subsonic flight regime above 200kts from zero g up to the angle of attack limit from low level up to 30,000ft. Similarly A03 had by the end of 1982 done most of its radar and weapon systems integration flight trials.

The ADV had different radar and weapons from the IDS because of its different role. The aircraft's primary armament consisted of four BAe Dynamics Skyflash air-to-air missiles under the fuselage. These missiles had replaced the earlier AIM7E–2 Sparrow on the Phantoms. The Skyflash was based on the body of the Sparrow but with an entirely new motor and seeker head. Four AIM9L Sidewinder air-to-air missiles were carried for shorter range engagements while a single 27mm IWKA Mouser revolver cannon was included for very close range work. This weapon is housed in the starboard lower fuselage. The space that was normally occupied by a second cannon in the IDS variant is taken up by additional avionics that were made homeless by the installation of a built-in refuelling probe in the port upper forward fuselage. In addition to its extra internal fuel over the IDS the F MK3 also has a much larger 495 imp. gall. auxiliary fuel tank, one carried on each of the inboard underwing pylons. These pylons have been fitted with stub pylons able to carry an AIM9L on each side of the fuel tank.

For the future the F3 will probably adopt the US built AIM 120 AMRAAM active air-to-air missile as a Skyflash replacement, although at the time of writing both the BAe Active Skyflash and S225X missiles were possible contenders. AMRAAM is a fire-and-forget weapon, unlike the Skyflash which has to have the

The first two prototypes were painted in a smart black and white scheme as here on ZA254. (BAe)

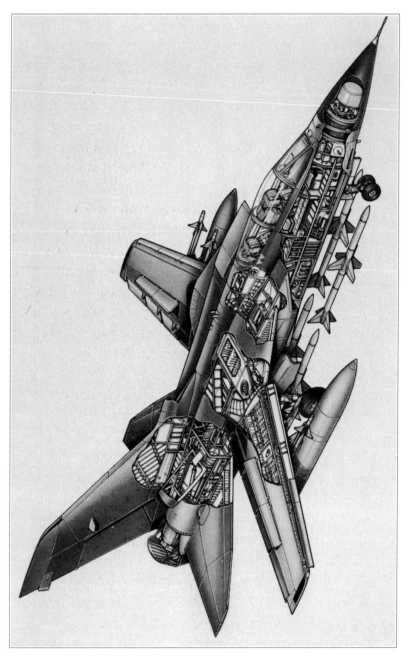

A cutaway view of the Tornado ADV. (BAe)

target painted by the Foxhunter radar throughout the engagement, thus leaving the Tornado vulnerable to attack by enemy fighters. It was expected that the Sidewinder would be replaced in the F3 force by the AIM132 ASRAAM short range missile but in 1992 the MOD announced that this weapon would be adopted only by the Harrier GR7 and EF 2000 as Tornado F3 is to be replaced by EF 2000. With the introduction of EF 2000 still seven or more years distant it still remains possible that ASRAAM will be issued to F3 squadrons.

The Tornado F3's already impressive weapons load can be enhanced still further with the activation of the outboard underwing pylons which are not used at present. This would allow the aircraft to carry say four AMRAAMs under the fuselage, four Sidewinders or ASRAAMS on the normal inboard underwing pylons, along with the two drop tanks, and a further two AMRAAMs on the outboard underwing pylons, giving a total of six BVR and four short range missiles. Alternatively the outboard underwing pylons could accommodate triple launchers for ASRAAM if this were adopted, allowing a further six missiles to be carried for a total of fourteen AAMs true combat persistence.

The main changes between the Tornado IDS and ADV are internally, with the aircraft sharing 80% commonality with each other. Among the external changes was the ADV having a 4ft 5$\frac{1}{2}$in (1.36m) fuselage extension resulting in a more pointed nose. This allowed an extra bay forward of the wings, and also allowed the aircraft to carry four Skyflash medium range air-to-air missiles under its fuselage with the front pair being semi-recessed. Another of the offsets was the ability to carry additional internal fuel.

The Tornado ADV also has a second INS to compensate for the loss of the doppler velocity sensing radar used on the GR MK1 for basic navigation information. The INS is autonomous in operation in that it requires no external inputs apart from feeding in the aircraft's precise position at the start of each flight. It does however suffer from slippage, creating positional errors over say a two hour sortie therefore the Tornado crew must update the system with fixes throughout the flight.

The variable geometry wings are of all-metal construction, the fixed inboard section has a 60° sweepback on the IDS variant and 67° of sweepback on the ADV; the outer movable section can be swept from the 25° fully forward position to the 67° fully swept position. The wing has no ailerons but has two spoilers in the upper surface forward of the trailing edge. These augment roll control at intermediate and fully forward wing sweep. The entire outer edge of the wing trailing edge with the exception of the wing tips, incorporates full span, fixed vein, double slotted fowler flaps in four sections, while the wing leading edge has three slats. Although the wings of both variants are basically the same, the F MK3 does have auto wing sweep facility with four pre-programmed settings: 25° fully forward for speeds up to Mach 0.73, 45° for speeds up to Mach 0.88, 58° speeds up to Mach 0.95, and the fully swept position of 67° for speeds up Mach 2.2.

The landing gear consists of a hydraulically retractable tricycle unit. Dunlop wheels with multi-disc brakes carry low pressure heavy duty tyres and Goodyear anti-skid units allowing operations from semi-prepared surfaces.

The fuselage is of all-metal, semi monocoque construction, which is built in three separate sections. The front fuselage and rear fuselage are built by BAe. The upper rear fuselage has two large door type airbrakes that are extended by hydraulic jacks; they form part of the skin on each side of the upper rear fuselage. The Tornado has a built-in arrester hook in the rear fuselage, this can help if the aircraft is forced to land within a very short distance,

ZE789 AU/56R Squadron lands after a display at Leuchars, keeping the nose up as long as possible as part of the display. (Hugh Harkins)

This aircraft shows the amount of moving surfaces on the wings when landing. (Hugh Harkins)

for example a damaged runway. The centre section, including the intakes and wing pivoting mechanism, is built by MBB. The fuselage houses most of the aircraft's fuel in Uniroyal, multi-cell, self-sealing integral tanks. Other fuel tanks are located in the wings and the tail fin. Refuelling is accomplished through a standard NATO single point pressure connector. The Tornado has a fuel jettison pipe on the fin trailing edge above the rudder.

The swept tail unit is of cantilever all-metal construction and comprises a single, broad chord, swept twin spar tailfin, with rudder mounting with low set all-moving horizontal surfaces called tailerons. The tailerons and rudder are actuated by electrically controlled hydraulic jacks, and operate in unison for pitch control or differentially for roll control.

The one piece cockpit canopy opens upwards and is hinged at the rear. The steeply raked windscreen built by Lucas Aerospace comprises a flat centre panel and two curved side panels which are heavily armoured in order to meet the RAF's strict bird-strike requirements. Sierracotte electrical conductive heating is incorporated in the entire windscreen, this is effective for anti-icing and demisting. The windscreen is kept free of water by rain dispersal ducts which bleed hot pressurized air from the aircraft's air-conditioning system. The whole windscreen area hinges forward, allowing access to the pilot's instrument panel and the Head Up Display (HUD). Beneath the canopy the two crew members sit on Martin Baker MK10A zero zero ejection seats. In the case of ejection an MDC in the canopy detonates to shatter the canopy a split second before the seat fires.

As with the Tornado aircraft the engine that was to power it was to be a Tri-National project with Rolls Royce, MTU and Fiat's engine division, all joining together to form Turbo Union and manufacture the Rolls Royce RB199 turbofan engine. The first eighteen Tornados ADVs were F MK2s, these had the original RB199 MK 103 turbofan engine as fitted in the IDS, itself an uprated version of the MK101, but the difinitive F MK3 version from ZE154 onwards had the uprated MK104 with a thrust 10% more than the 103 along with a more efficient fuel consumption. This power plant introduces a 14in (36cm) jet pipe extension for an extra afterburner section, giving an extra 450lb (2kn) thrust over the MK103.

The MK104 also introduces Digital Engine Control Unit (DECU) which is a replacement for the analogue mechanical system used in earlier versions of the RB199. This system allows better control over the engine, is more reliable and incorporates built-in test equipment.

The RB199 is in the same class as the American J79 turbojet which powers such aircraft as the F4 Phantom II, and the F404 turbofan engine. The J79 which is an old design is 208in (530cm) long and weighs in at 3,847lb (1745kg) while the F404 is 159in (403cm) long and weighs 2,000lb (908kg). Turbo Union was able to go one better by producing an engine only 127in (324cm) long and weighing 1,980lb (900kg).

The RB199's small size is due to the use of three shafts, each of which is free to rotate at the speed best suited to the part of the engine mounted on it. The outer shaft carries the LP fan and is driven by a two stage turbine. The middle turbine rotates in the opposite direction and carries a three stage compressor and a single stage turbine. The inner shaft, which rotates in the same direction as the outer, has a six stage compressor whose final stages are made of heat resistant alloy rather than titanium which is used in the other stages, along with the blades for the IP compressor and LP fan. The HP shaft is driven by a single stage turbine and is able to take 1,327° Centigrade from the annular combustion

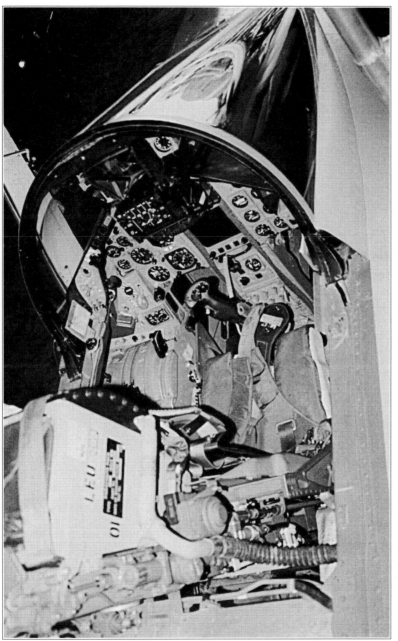

The Tornado ADV cockpit was designed before the change to Glass cockpit technology with multi-function TV screens as in the F15E or EFA 2000. The HUD provides all the vital flight information and target engagement parameters while a head-down screen shows the radar and navigation displays from the rear cockpit. (Hugh Harkins)

The AI24 Foxhunter radar is the eyes and ears of the F3.

chamber. The after-burner is a compact unit and has no area where core gas and by-pass air can mix, the two mixtures are burned concurrently.

The Tornado was one of the first combat aircraft in the world to dispense with the traditional braking parachute and instead use thrust reversers. In the Tornado the thrust reverse buckets are just aft of the after-burner and deploy as soon as the wheels hit the ground and the spoilers come out; after deploying, the thrust reversers allow the Tornado to land in a very short distance for a front line fighter.

The Tornado ADV has the GR MK1's Texas Instruments radar replaced with the GEC Avionics AI24 Foxhunter radar. Most of the early problems have now been solved with the RAF's Tornados all at least to Stage One standard. The Foxhunter operates in the I band using a pulse doppler technique known as Frequency Modulated Interrupted Continuous Wave. The advanced cassegrain antenna gives a good performance even in a high clutter or jamming environment.

The GEC Marconi AI24 Foxhunter underwent continuous de-lays, resulting in the F MK2 entering service much later than was originally planned. The first Foxhunters were taken aloft in a converted Canberra and Buccaneer before finally on 17 June 1981, after almost a year of delays, the third Prototype, ZA283, took to the air with a Foxhunter set installed. By March 1983 this aircraft was on its third version of the Foxhunter which was known as the B series. The first of 20 pre-production radars was delivered in July 1983. It was planned for the first production F MK2s to roll off the Warton production line with Foxhunters fitted later that year. As it was the F MK2 started delivery to the RAF from November 1984 without radars, instead the aircraft were delivered with lead ballast (known as Blue Circle radar) in their noses. Aircraft did not leave the Warton production line with Foxhunters until the middle of 1985.

After the initial contract and specification of Foxhunter had been agreed the RAF requested greater capability; this resulted in early radar sets being delivered below the specification required for operational service contributing to the many delays encountered with the equipment. Originally the RAF had not required a tail chase capability. Other shortcomings were large sidelobes which increased vulnerability to jamming, along with a below standard multi-mode tracking capability. The specification had called for 20 aircraft to be tracked while the radar continued to scan. As a result of the shortcomings GEC began a three year period of improvements that would bring all radars up to an acceptable standard by the early 1990s.

The delivery of radars was AI24 Foxhunter Type W 70 built for the sixty-two Block 8–10 aircraft, Type Z 80 built for eighty Block 11–12, while the final 76 Foxhunters, 50 for 46 RAF F3s, and 26 for 24 Royal Saudi Air Force F3s, were delivered to Stage 1 standard. The original Type Z radars were produced to meet ASR 395 meeting the RAF's original specifications before additional capabilities were requested. As the Type W was below even this original standard all but 26 sets have been upgraded to Type Z in a programme which began in 1988. The Type Z sets introduced improvements including increased detection range and tracking capability. The Stage One standard of radar comes closest to meeting the RAF's specification and introduces software improvements which give a much better close combat capability and improved ECCM Electronic Counter Measures. New Stage One Foxhunter began manufacture in September 1988, with 124 Type Zs, some of which were modified from Type W, also being brought up to this standard.

For close-in engagements the F3 has four AIM9L/M Sidewinder short range AAMs. (Hugh Harkins)

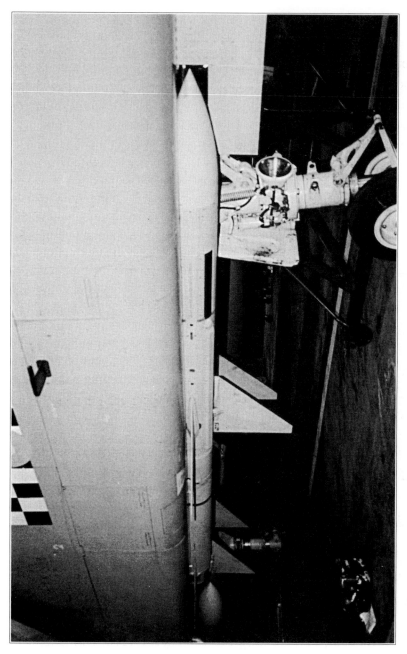

The cutting edge of the F3 is the medium range BAe Dynamics Skyflash AAM. (Hugh Harkins)

The AI24 Foxhunter uses a technique known as Frequency Modulated Interrupted Continuous Wave (FMICW), with which is integrated a Cossor IFF–3500 interrogator with a radar signal processor to suppress ground clutter (this was one of the problems associated with the radar's long development). Foxhunter's High Pulse Repetition Frequency (PRF) allows it to detect targets at an initial range of 100nm while the FMICW allows the target's range to be determined from the frequency range between transmission and reception.

As the targets are detected they are then stored in the central digital computer. Since the radar continues to scan normally the targets are unaware that they are the subject of detailed analysis. The whole system rejects unwanted signals, leaving only real targets which are then passed through the radar data processor before display to the aircraft crew. While the radar keeps up a running commentary on ranges, velocities and tracks of established targets, it continues to scan the area for additional targets.

While the RAF is now receiving satisfaction from its improved Foxhunters it was revealed that at one point the MOD almost cancelled the system and ordered the same firm's Blue Vixen radar developed for the Sea Harrier FA2.

One Tornado F2 ZD902 has the GEC Sensors Infra Red Search and Track (IRST) system installed, this system allows the aircraft to track its target while at the same time not alerting the enemy on its RWR. It is unlikely to be adopted on service aircraft in the current political climate but could feature in an F3 upgrade if EF 2000 encounters further service entry delays.

The original Tornado GR MK1 had an Elettronica ARI 23284 Radar Warning Receiver (RWR), the F MK3 has the more capable Marconi Space and Defence Systems Hermes modular Radar Warning and Homing Receiver (RHWR). The antennae for this are mounted on the upper fin trailing edge, and on the aircraft's wingtips. In the cockpit of both crew members the threats are displayed aurally and on the CRTs. The threats are then analysed, classified and displayed in alpha numeric form with accurate range and bearing of the threats. This is then compared with the Foxhunter radar target tracks, therefore allowing the crew to classify and allocate priority to any potential threats. The system can act passively or can burn through enemy jamming.

The RAF is patiently awaiting the arrival of the Stage Two radar upgrade from AA to AB standard which was due about now but has been put back to a future date. This will further the fighter's capabilities by the addition of a new processor giving automatic target acquisition and tracking and discrimination between head on targets by analysis of the radar signature of their first and second stage compressor blades.

Another system on the horizon is JTIDS or Joint Tactical Information Distribution System which will provide the Tornado F3 crew with an up to date picture on the entire air battle. It will also allow the F3 to contribute its own information, such as fuel and weapon states, back to their tactical H.Q. JTIDS provides the F3s and other friendly forces with a secure jam resistant communication network that can operate in a dense ECM environment. The system which is manufactured by Singer Kearfott and Rockwell Collins in the US and GEC Marconi in the UK, allows secure voice communications, accurate navigation and identification of friend or foe. The second production F MK3 ZE155 was held back on the production line until it flew on 16 October 1986 with a JTIDS Class 2 terminal installed; the initial flight trials took place in January 1987 when the aircraft established successful secure voice-free text and fixed format communications with a ground based terminal. The aircraft went to Yuma Arizona USA for the best part of the year undergoing trials.

The introduction of JTIDS has begun, starting with aircraft serialled from ZG751 to ZH559, all will initially be based at Coningsby before allocation to other squadrons. A further step towards operational service occurred during August 1994 when four Tornado F3s from the F3 OEU and 5 Squadron Coningsby together with an E3D Sentry from 8 Squadron Waddington with AAR support from a Tristar K1 of 216 Squadron Brize Norton deployed to Mountain Home AFB Idaho USA. The aim of the three week deployment was to test the inter-operability of JTIDS between different aircraft types. The USAF participation came from the 390FS F15Cs. This unit is the only Squadron in the USAF equipped with JTIDS, an E3A and the 389FS F16Cs Hill AFB which provided the adversary support. During the second week the USN provided an E2C Hawkeye AWACS and three F14D Tomcats from Miramar. Like the Stage Two radar upgrade, once introduced JTIDS will allow the RAF's Tornado F3s and Sentry AEW MK1s to defend the UK's airspace from attack into the year 2000 and beyond. The RAF took delivery of its last Tornado F3 ZH559 in March 1993; this was one of eight originally ordered for the Oman Air Force.

F3s are to be equipped with Vinten VICON 78 series 600 underfuselage flare dispensers and Bofers Phimat BOL304 chaff dispensers in the rear of the Sidewinder rails.

From the end of the decade the Tornado F3 will be supplanted by the EF 2000, although whether it is to be completely replaced is still open to speculation. Ideally it would be better to leave some F3s, some of which will be barely 10 years old, in the bomber destroyer role leaving the EF 2000s to concentrate on the fighters as well as hacking down the bombers. Other roles to which the Tornado F3 would be ideally suited include the maritime role of anti-shipping strike using the Sea Eagle ASM. This role is being taken over by the Tornado GR MK1B, but the F3's longer range would make it an ideal candidate for the future. Moreover, converting a few dozen redundant airframes to the Wild Weasel defence suppression role using the Air Launched Anti Radar (ALARM) Missile would make sense, the Saudi Air Force has already expressed interest in converting their 24 ADVs to the Wild Weasel role.

Studies were carried out during 1988 into the effects of fitting General Electric F404 engines and the Hughes APG-65 into a Tornado ADV. The results showed that in many respects it would be inferior to an FA18 Hornet therefore the whole idea was dropped. Two years later the idea was again resurrected, this time using EJ200 engines and the ECR-90 radar currently being developed for the EF 2000. Unfortunately this solution was calculated to be deficient by a wide margin when compared to the projected performance of EF 2000, with fleet effectives being 2.35 Tornados to 1 EF 2000. When designing the EJ200 powerplant for EFA Eurojet was asked that it be retrofittable in Tornado. The dry thrust of an EJ200 is almost equivalent to the afterburning thrust of an RB199, 13,490lb to 9,656lb and 20,230lb to 16,920lb. The extra thrust would improve Tornado's dash speed acceleration initial climb rate and give extra power for combat manoeuvring. Unfortunately the decision to replace the F3 force with EF 2000 from the end of the decade means it is unlikely that the F3 will receive the EJ200 installation on cost grounds. When the Tornado programme was launched it was referred to as the MRCA, this has proved to be a false claim with three separate versions of the IDS variant in RAF service all for different roles along with the F3 for its designed role. An upgrade of some F3s to say F/A3

One of the main external differences between the F2 and the F3 is the former having an extra 14 in. tail pipe extension. (Hugh Harkins)

A 617 Squadron Tornado GR1 in formation with an F3 of 11 Squadron. (BAe)

The F3's successor will be the Eurofighter 2000 second prototype DA2 ZH588 seen here  at Warton. As the EF2000 project gets underway F3s will probably be involved in ECR-90 radar development trials acting as targets and chase planes. (BAe)

standard, replacing the Foxhunter radar with the Blue Vixen multi-role radar as installed in the Sea Harrier F/A2, Forward Looking Infra Red (FLIR) and the Spartan Terrain Reference Terrain Following Navigation System as originally planned for the Tornado GR4 upgrade would turn the ADV into a true MRCA. The USN has already demonstrated what can be done with their F14D Tomcats which now increasingly employ air-to-ground weapons.

Whatever the future has in store for the Tornado F3 after the introduction of EF 2000 one thing is sure, despite the bad and one must say ill-informed press the aircraft has had recently, the Tornado F MK3 has been and will remain one of if not the finest of the world's long range interceptors for the foreseeable future.

# 2

# Tornado in Service

The first production Tornado, F2 ZD899, flew at Warton for the first time on 12 April 1984 although it was the second production, F2 ZD900, that was the first to fly on 5.3.84. The first aircraft to enter RAF service was ZD901 which joined 229 OCU on 5 November 1984. The F2 was an interim model and only 18 were built with the last being delivered to the OCU in October 1985. The first standard production F3, ZE154, took to the air on 20.11.85 and entered service in 1986, initially with the OCU then with 29 Squadron in January 1987. This was not the first F3 to fly, that honour going to ZE155 which took to the air on 16.10.85. The main improvements of the F3 over the F2 are the ability to carry four underwing Sidewinders, the addition of auto wing sweep facility and the more powerful RB199 MK104 engines.

Of course throughout its service life the F3 has been further improved, most notably in the capability of the radar software. With the delivery of the F3 well under way it was decided to retire the F2 with the first going to RAF St Athan for storage in March 1986 and the last in January 1988. It was planned to upgrade the F2s to F2A standard which would be identical to the F3 except for the engines, but with the disbandment of 23 Squadron and the entry into RAF service of eight aircraft originally ordered by Oman, it was decided in mid 1993 to scrap 12 of the F2s: ZD901, ZD903, ZD904, ZD905, ZD932, ZD933, ZD934, ZD936,

ZD937, ZD938, ZD940 and ZD941 which were languishing in storage at RAF St Athan, therefore this plan will now not go ahead.

All three Tornado ADV prototypes as well as three F2s that escaped storage are involved in trials and experimental work with the DRA A&AEE and BAe.

The DRA Farnborough operates Tornado F2A(T) TIARA, Tornado Integrated Avionics Research Aircraft, ZD902. This aircraft has a GEC Ferranti Blue Vixen radar designed for the RN Sea Harrier FAZ2 installed in place of its Foxhunter Stage 2G. This system is supplemented by a GEC sensors Infra Red Search and Track System, IRST. The front cockpit has been modified to simulate a state of the art single seat fighter complete with a holographic HUD, three full-colour multi function Cathode Ray Tube cockpit displays as well as other advanced systems such as Hands on Throttle and Stick (HOTAS) control system and JTIDS. The aircraft also has the ability to use a Helmet Mounted Sight (HMS). This aircraft also features modified underfuselage fuel tanks which house various trials equipment, they can be fitted with either a high speed or low speed nose cone. The aircraft was seen in the static park at the 1994 Farnborough show with a modified tank with an optical window to house Forward Looking Infra Red (FLIR). ZD902 was still at Farnborough in late 1994 but is due to move to Bascombe Down to join the rest of the DRA fleet. Unfortunately there are no current plans to upgrade the RAF's F3 force with these features although with further delays of EF2000 it remains a slim possibility.

ZD902 is available for lease to firms in the private sector requiring airborne tests of equipment for modern combat aircraft, and for such is equipped with full on-board recording facilities to enable easy analysis of the results of each flight.

ZE759 BT 29 Squadron flying over Sydney Harbour Bridge during Australia's Bicentennial celebrations in 1988. (BAe)

The first and third prototypes, ZA254 AO1, ZA283 AO3 and a pair of F2s ZD899T and ZD939, are involved with Tornado ADV radar development trials flying from BAe Warton. Most of the radar development support is provided by BAe on the MOD's behalf, but the whole programme is heavily reliant on GEC Marconi whose personnel are completely integrated within the test programme. The main targets for this programme were until recently a handful of BAC Lightning F3s and F6s, although other aircraft types were regularly flown in the trials as well. The main objective of the test programme is to demonstrate the AI24 Foxhunter radar's ability to track one or more targets in a multitude of engagement scenarios from high to low level, fast or slow or against sophisticated ECM jamming.

The second prototypes, ZA267 and F2 ZD900, are used by the A&AEE Bascombe Down as trials aircraft.

By June 1992 it was rumoured that the Tornado F2s in storage at RAF St Athan were to be leased to the RMAF pending a possible sale of EFAs. The UK MOD was reported to have offered the lease of RAF Tornado F2s in store at RAF St Athan to the Malaysian Air Force under a Government-to-Government MoU. The Malaysian requirement was for up to 24 fighters although there are only 15 F2s in storage, with the 3 remaining F2s along with all 3 prototypes all involved in various trials with BAe, the DRA and the A&AEE. Such rumours were put to an end by the Malaysian announcement that it was to purchase a mix of Mig 29s and FA18 Hornets.

Once in squadron service the F3 began to earn the respect of its crews, especially in February 1987 when the F3 made its debut on the Aberporth ranges, achieving outstanding results in test firing of the Skyflash missile. By June 1987 29 Squadron was involved in exercise Central Enterprise.

ZE155 of the A&AEE Bascombe Down was the first F3 to cross the Atlantic, supported by a Tristar K MK1 of 216 Squadron in September 1987. This was followed later in the month by the first unrefuelled crossing of the Atlantic by a British fighter when the same aircraft returned to the UK after completing tropical weather trials in Arizona USA. The distance covered was 2,200 nautical miles from Canada in a time of 4 hours and 45 minutes.

The Tornado F3 has practised interceptions against most NATO combat types but the following is an account of one of the more unusual types of aircraft to be involved in a practice intercept.

The flight was controlled by Warton Air Traffic Control. Visual contact was obtained at about 12 miles and the two aircraft joined at the pre-briefed position to the north of the Mull of Galloway. This allowed both aircraft to fly directly on the supersonic bravo run at FL330–33,000ft.

It was one of the most realistic interception sorties ever flown by a supersonic fighter, in this case the Tornado F2. The target was one of the few aircraft that could give the fighter a run for its money – Concorde.

Having joined into close formation, the two aircraft were positioned on the supersonic run by Warton ATC and given clearance to accelerate. At 1.2 IMN height was increased to 37,000ft. This speed and height gave the Tornado room to position around the Concorde and carry out the photographic mission.

Both aircraft accelerated to supersonic flight together, the Tornado positioned behind to the right and left of the Concorde. As the fighter came abeam the cockpit of the BA SST, the only effect of M1 flight was a little lateral buffeting. This was due to the transition through the major shock wave or sound barrier.

Later in the flight the captain of Concorde noted the same effect as the Tornado flew ahead, although the shock waves were

ZE209 from 56R Squadron awaits its next sortie with its cockpit canopy open. (Hugh Harkins)

ZE293 HT leaving its HAS at Leuchars for a sortie on 6 September 1993. (Hugh Harkins)

This formation of Tornados, foreground, and Phantoms, background, marked the disbandment of 56 Phantom Squadron and the formation of 56R Tornado Squadron. (BAe)

ZE161 FG 25 Squadron RAF Leeming. (Hugh Harkins)

not visible, of course. The supersonic photographic flight was terminated after about ten minutes, during which the Tornado and Concorde had covered 138 miles.

Unofficially formed at RAF Coningsby on 1 November 1984, No 229 OCU received its first F2s on 5 November when ZD901 and ZD903 landed at the station. Official formation date was 1 May 1985 and the unit was immediately in the limelight when one of its aircraft was put on the airshow circuit, flying a synchronised display with a Spitfire of the Battle of Britain Memorial Flight. 229 received its full complement of 16 F2s when the last arrived on 21 October 1985. Also on this day the F2 was involved in its first Air Defence exercise, Priory 85/2. Delivery of Tornado F MK3s began with the arrival of ZE159 on 28 July 1986. With the introduction to service of the improved F MK3 the F MK2s were gradually withdrawn and put into storage at RAF St Athan.

The OCU runs two different courses, the long course is for aircrews with no air defence experience and lasts for six months, during which pilots receive 61.35 hours and navigators 48.45 hours. The short course lasts only three months with pilots receiving 60 hours and navigators 48.55. Although this may seem the same as the long course only in a shorter time it is not, because unlike the long course, pilots and navigators fly as a crew for most of the time instead of with an instructor as on the long course. The OCU in fact can claim to be the first operational front line F3 Squadron as the unit was assigned the 65R Squadron number plate on 1 January 1987 even before 29 Squadron had formed.

On 6 February 1992 a Tornado F3 ZE794 A4 of 229 OCU 65R Squadron visited Duxford for the roll out of restored Hunter F6A XE627 in 65 Squadron colours. Following this the unit disbanded in July 1992 and was replaced by the Tornado F3 OCU which adopted the 56R Squadron number plate.

No 29 Squadron stood down with its Phantom FGR2 fighters on 1 December 1986 and was declared operational on the Tornado F3 on 1 November 1987. 29 Squadron has since 1 January 1988 been assigned to SACLANT for maritime defence of the fleet. The Squadron also has an out of NATO area commitment and for this reason it was chosen for Operation Golden Eagle, a circumnavigation of the world, between 21 August and 26 October 1988. During this four aircraft participated in a Malaysian AD exercise as well as visiting some SE Asia air forces and flying at airshows in Australia as part of the Bicentenary celebrations.

No 5 Squadron was the second to form on the F3 and the first to convert from Lightnings. The Squadron formed on 1 January 1988 at Coningsby although its first aircraft, ZE292 arrived at the station on 25 September 1987. No 5 Squadron participated in the Malaysian AD exercise in 1990. A pair of 5 Squadron Tornado F3s, ZG730 CC and ZG735 CO, provided an escort for British Airways Boeing 757 G-BIKO on July 8 1992 during part of the airliner's flight from Heathrow to Newcastle. The reason for the special treatment was that the 757 was the five millionth movement handled by the RAF Eastern radar. This unit was established in 1965 with type 82 radar at Watton, before moving to West Drayton in 1989. It now receives inputs from the CAA's civilian radar network.

The Seed trophy for 1989/90 was awarded to No 5 Squadron. This is given to the squadron in 11 Group which achieves the best air-to-air gunnery results. 5 Squadron flew a farewell formation for the Shackleton when F3s, ZE254 CA and ZE730 CC, flew in formation with Shackleton AEW, MK2 and the first Sentry AEW MK1 ZH102 to be delivered to the RAF.

The first F3, ZE764, for No 11 Squadron arrived at Coningsby on 25 April 1988. Here 11D Squadron came into existence on 1

Only 43 years separate first flights of the Spitfire and the Tornado ADV. (Hugh Harkins)

For its 75th anniversay 111 Squadron decorated aircraft ZG 776. (Hugh Harkins)

The 1994 56R Squadron display ship ZE789 AU landing after a display. Note the deflection angle of the all-moving tailplane. (Hugh Harkins)

F3s ZE858 GO 43 Squadron foreground and ZE835 HK 111 Squadron background escort Russian Tu95 Bear 20 to the IAT at RAF Fairford on 21.7.93. (Crown Copyright)

May. On 1 July 1988 the Squadron officially formed on the F3, at the same time the Squadron was moved to its new home of RAF Leeming to begin formation of the Leeming wing. 11 Squadron Tornado F3 commenced their work-up flights on 1 July 1988. After a six month work-up 11 was declared operational and assigned to SACLANT on 1 November 1988.

On 1 November the second of the wing's Tornado F3 units was formed, No 23 Squadron, with the first of this squadron's aircraft arriving on 5 August. 23 Squadron F3s made the first live interception of a Soviet aircraft actually two Bear Ds of a Leeming based Tornado F3 on 10 November 1989 over the Norwegian Sea.

23 Squadron started its work-up on 4 January 1989. This was completed on 3 July. After a seven month work-up 23 was declared operational and assigned to SACUER on 1 August 1989.

During late 1989 the squadron sent detachments to Germany, France and Belgium. In January 1990 the Leeming wing took over the QRA for the Northern Sector to allow the Leuchars wing to concentrate on conversion to the Tornado F MK3. The Q commitment was handed back to Leuchars in January 1992. In 1990 the Squadron went to Italy, the Netherlands and Denmark, before deploying to RAF Valley for the MPC. As is already explained 25 Squadron contributed air and ground crews as part of 11 Composite Squadron deployed to Saudi Arabia following the Iraq invasion of Kuwait.

In 1992 the Squadron deployed to Valley once again for missile firings, followed by a deployment to Sardinia to use the Deccimommannu ACMI against RN Sea Harrier FRS1s. Later in the year the unit deployed some personnel to Goose Bay Canada along with commitment to the Falklands. After a stint of duty flying the Air Exclusion Zone over Bosnia as part of operation

Deny Flight the MOD announced on 7 July 1993 that 23 Squadron was to disband as part of the February defence cuts, with final disbandment taking place on 23 March 1994.

To complete the Leeming wing No 25 Squadron was formed at Leeming on 1 October 1989. This unit's last equipment was the Bloodhound SAM until it was disbanded on 30 September 1989. The first F3 for 25 Squadron came to the base almost a year before when ZE858 arrived on 15 December 1988.

25 Squadron was chosen to provide the solo Tornado F3 display crew and aircraft for the 1991 and 1992 display seasons. For the 1991 season the display aircraft was ZE167 FO which was painted in its 75th anniversary markings which consisted of black wing leading and trailing edges, black fin with large white middle section, white upper fuselage with black cheat lines along upper sides. The lower fuselage sides had a white stripe with black cheat lines either side.

43 Squadron, the Fighting Cocks, was the next squadron to form and also the first of the Leuchars wing. ZE963 arrived for ground familiarities on 23 August and the first two aircraft for the Squadron ZE961 and ZE962, arrived very publicly during the annual Battle of Britain At Home day on 23 September 1989. Partnering 43 in policing the Northern sector of the UKADR is No 111 Squadron which formed on the type on 1 May 1990.

In July 1992 No 1435 Flight in the Falkland Islands became a Tornado F MK3 operator when it discarded its Phantom FGR2s for the type. The need for a fighter presence in the Falklands has remained unaltered since the end of the conflict with Argentina in 1982 and as that country does not seem ready to drop its claim of sovereignty over the islands the Tornados will remain as a deterrent to any further invasion plans the Argentinians may have.

ZE858 A5 landing at Coningsby while serving with the OCU. (Hugh Harkins)

Air defence team for the 1990s:
the Tornado F3 and Boeing E3D Sentry AEW Mk1. (BAe)

ZE292 AU of 65R Squadron at the Scottish International Airshow Prestwick Airport 6.6.92. (Hugh Harkins)

The four Tornados are based at RAF Mount Pleasant on East Falkland.

Three Tornado F3s, ZE209, ZE790 and ZE792, departed RAF Coningsby on 6 July 1992 bound for the Falklands to replace the Phantoms of 1435 flight. Later a further three, including ZE758, which received the code letter C, also left for Mount Pleasant.

All F3 Squadrons usually spend a month at RAF Akrotiri Cyprus for the annual APC and three weeks per year at Deci using the NATO funded ACMI range where the results of each engagement are recorded on an instrumentation pod which is fitted to the aircraft. During each operational tour each crew has the opportunity to fire at least one Skyflash and one Sidewinder at the Missile Practice Camp (MPC) at RAF Valley, Wales. The aircraft transit to the Aberporth ranges for the firings.

As previously mentioned, No 23 Squadron at RAF Leeming was disbanded in February 1994; this left the RAF with only six front line fighter Squadrons along with the F3 OCU. With the announcement of the scrapping of 14 further F3s which were damaged during maintenance work by Airwork and the leasing of 24 aircraft to the Italian Air Force it seems that a further disbandment of at least one Squadron is likely, of the others all will continue to fly the Tornado F3 until the advent of the much delayed and much troubled EF 2000 which should enter service at the end of the decade.

# 3

# Export

Although not the first export customer to order Tornados the Al Quwwat al Jawwiya as Saudiya (Royal Saudi Air Force RSAF) was the first customer to order both the IDS and ADV of the Tornado as well as being the first to receive export Tornados. The RSAF has a tradition of buying British military aircraft having previously received Strikemasters and Lightnings. On 26 September 1985 the Saudi Government signed an order for 48 Tornado IDS, equivalent to the RAF's GR MK1, and 24 ADV Tornados, equivalent to the RAF's F MK3. The agreement Al Yammanah I also included a pair of BAe Jetstreams fitted out as navigator trainers for both variants of the Tornado as well as 30 each of Pilatus PC9 turboprop trainers and BAe Hawk MK65 advanced trainers. It also called for early delivery of 20 aircraft, for this reason the RAF had to give up 18 of its final GR MK1s, with the other two aircraft originally laid down for West Germany. All these aircraft were originally in Batch 7 but were brought forward to be included in Batch 5.

The 24 Tornado ADVs for the RSAF were completed from the RAF's order included in Batch 6, all of which were single-stick aircraft although six were completed as twin-stickers to meet the RSAF order for six such aircraft, as the RAF was unwilling to part with any twin-stick aircraft. The RAF received ADVs from later batches to make up for the loss of its 24 aircraft. The first

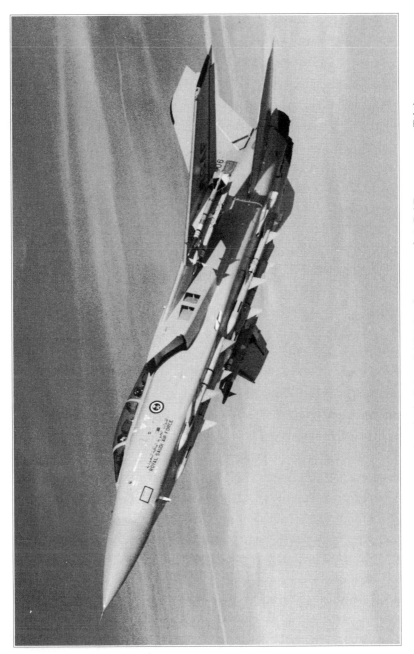

Saudi aircraft are armed with Skyflash and AIM9Ls, the same as their RAF counterparts. (BAe)

Tornado F MK3 for the RSAF was ZE859 with the Saudi serial 2905, and this flew for the first time on 1 December 1988, and was subsequently handed to the Saudis on 9 February 1989, before handover to the RSAF to equip 29 Squadron at Dharhan on 20 March 1989 along with three other aircraft. 29 Squadron had received its full complement of 12 F MK3s including four dual control aircraft by 20 September 1989.

The second Tornado ADV Squadron for the RSAF was 34 Squadron, also based at Dahrhan. This unit received its first aircraft on 14–15 November 1989, although it was initially assigned to co-located 29 Squadron. 34 Squadron finished its re-equipment in 1990.

RSAF Tornado F MK3s were the first to be fitted on the production line with the Stage One version of the AI24 Foxhunter radar having the specification called for by the RAF. In Squadron service Saudi Tornado F3s are essentially equipped the same as their RAF cousins with the primary armament of four BVR Skyflash air-to-air missiles complemented by four AIM9L Sidewinder AAMs. Both missile systems are backed up by a single 27mm Mouser cannon as on RAF aircraft. The Saudis use the same 2250 ltr (495imp gall.) external tanks as the RAF and these can be substituted with the 330 gall. tanks used by the IDS Tornados in Saudi service. The Saudis also adopted a similar overall air defence grey colour scheme for its F3s. Markings are carried in the shape of Saudi roundels on both sides of the forward fuselage and on the upper port wing and lower starboard wing USAF style. The starboard upper wing has the letters RSAF with the same on the port lower wing. RSAF Tornado F MK3 interceptors share their role with the McDonnell Douglas F15 Eagle.

Another Tornado sale to the RSAF under Al Yammanna II was provisionally agreed in July 1988 but was not formally signed

Final Tornado F3 on delivery to RAF, 1993. (BAe)

ZH554 GJ was one of the eight aircraft originally ordered by Oman but delivered to the RAF instead. (Hugh Harkins)

until May 1993. This order was originally for a further 12 IDS and 36 ADV but when signed it was altered to consist of 48 IDS Tornados along with a further batch of Hawk trainers.

The following is a full list of the 24 RSAF serials for its ADVs:

| | |
|---|---|
| 2901 (ZE861) | 2902 (ZE882) |
| 2903 (ZE882) | 2904 (ZE883) |
| 2905 (ZE884) | 2906 (ZE859) |
| 2907 (ZE860) | 2908 (ZE885) |
| 2909 (ZE886) | 2910 (ZE890) |
| 2911 (ZE891) | 2912 (ZE905) |
| 3451 (ZE909) | 3452 (ZE910) |
| 3453 (ZE912) | 3454 (ZE913) |
| 3455 (ZE914) | 3456 (ZE935) |
| 3457 (ZE937) | 3458 (ZE938) |
| 3459 (ZE939) | 3460 (ZE940) |
| 3461 (ZE943) | 3462 (ZE960) |

Of the above 2901–04 and 3451–52 were twin stick dual control aircraft although still retaining full operational capability like their RAF counterparts.

At the outbreak of hostilities between Iraq and Kuwait on 2 August 1990 the RSAF began mounting defensive CAPs south of the border with Kuwait and Iraq as it was unknown whether Iraq had further ambitions in the region. Sharing in these duties were the F15 Eagles of the RSAF 13 and 42 Squadrons. The Saudi Tornados and F15s were soon joined by American and British interceptors within a week or so. During Desert Shield the Saudi Tornado F MK3s worked closely with their RAF counterparts, both undertaking daily CAPs along with other Coalition fighters.

Once war came in January 1991 the F3s worked long hard hours in both defensive and offensive CAPs with the crews having

Tornado ADV 2906 of the Royal Saudi Air Force. (BAe)

no resulting air-to-air combats to show for their work. This was due to the fact that the Iraqi Air Force chose not to come up and face the allied fighters, instead they either fled to Iran or hid in their HAS (Hardened Air Shelter) to be destroyed by the attack strike aircraft.

The first customer for the Tornado ADV was the Al Quwwat al Jawwiya al Sultanat Oman, which ordered eight aircraft for the interception role in order to release the service's Jaguars currently employed on interception duties for the ground attack role. All the aircraft were to be dual control under an order placed on 14 August 1985. Deliveries were to have begun in 1988 but this date was put back to 1992 until the order was finally cancelled with the RAF taking delivery of the eight aircraft instead. The aircraft received the RAF serials ZH552-ZH559, with the last being delivered in March 1993.

By 1987 BAe was trying hard to interest the JASDF in the Tornado J, this would be jointly developed with the Japanese aircraft industry. The Tornado J was developed from the earlier Super Tornado which would use the ADV's fuselage but with IDS and ECR equipment included. If successful the Tornado J could have been used for the long range maritime attack with the Mitsubishi ASM-1 anti-ship missile but would have retained full interception capability.

To demonstrate the feasibility of such an aircraft the third ADV prototype ZA283 had its outboard underwing stations activated, and flew a series of demonstration sorties but the Tornado J came to nothing.

In June 1993 the Italian AF announced that it would like to buy or lease existing fighters from some of its NATO allies in order to counter the potential air threat from Serbia. For this the Italian AF currently relies on obsolescent F104S Starfighters which

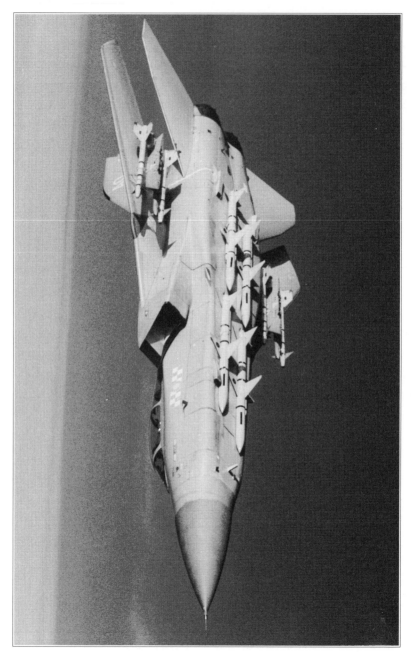

Italian AF crews will undergo conversion training to the Tornado F3 with 56R Squadron at Coningsby. (BAe)

are to be replaced by EF 2000s at the end of the century. As EFA is still at least seven years away from entering service the Italians want an interim fighter to plug the gap. Front runners were surplus USAF F15 and F16 fighters and Tornado F3s made surplus by defence cuts. It would appear more realistic for the Italian AF to adopt the US fighters as they are single crew aircraft, as is the F104. On the other hand the Italians already operate the Tornado IDS strike variant and therefore have air and ground crews with considerable Tornado experience.

The requirement was for up to 50 aircraft and the USAF offered 70 F15s and F16s for lease or sale. The RAF on the other hand would be severely overstretched to maintain the current proposed six squadrons and an OCU as well as an out of area flight in the Falklands if it were to part with 50 of its F3 force.

On 6 November 1993 the Italian Defence Minister, Fabio Fabri, while on a visit to London announced that the Tornado F3 had been selected as the Air Force's stopgap fighter pending the introduction of EFA 2000 early in the next century. On 21 March 1994 it was revealed that the UK MOD had held discussions with their Italian counterparts in connection with the lease of 24 (not the 50 previously mentioned) Tornado F3s over a ten year period.

By March 1994 it was decided that 120 Groupo (360 Stormo at Gio-del-Colle) and 180 Groupo (370 Stormo at Trapani/Birgi) would be the units to re-equip with Tornado F3s. Unusually it was also announced that the aircraft would be crewed by two pilots who would alternate between the front and rear cockpits. The Italians will undergo conversion training with the RAF's Tornado F3 OCU (56R Squadron) at RAF Coningsby. The first batch of 12 aircraft is due to be delivered to Gio in the third quarter of 1995 after which the remaining 12 will be delivered to Trapani. Included in the deal is the lease of 96 Skyflash SARH missiles as the main armament for the F3s, putting to rest rumours that the aircraft would be modified to fire the Aspide SARHM as used on the F104S Starfighters.

That the Tornado ADV was not an outstanding export success story was no fault of the aircraft itself but rather a combination of politics, high price (current flyaway price about £22M) and the complexity of the design. Most Western influenced nations went instead for cheaper, simpler and less capable designs such as the US Lockheed F16 Fighting Falcon. Indeed, together with the F15 Eagle and the FA18 Hornet, the US manufactures had the Western influenced fighter market cornered from the early 1980s, with such large home production runs allowing lower unit costs and in some cases the US Government offering huge industrial offsets.

Even on this side of the Atlantic BAe negotiated sales of the two seat Hawk 100 advanced trainer and Hawk 200 single seat fighter to the Omani Air Force at the expense of the contract for eight Tornado F MK3s mentioned above. If all goes according to plan, which seems doubtful, the RAF will begin replacement of the Tornado F MK3 with EF 2000s from the year 2000. This will leave a lot of surplus aircraft with a very low number of hours available for sale or lease on the second-hand fighter market, although once again even larger quantities of US F15s and F16s surplus to US requirements would mean the Tornado is yet again in for some tough sales battles in the future.

In an attempt to interest export customers such as the JASDF the second Tornado ADV prototype demonstrated the aircraft's anti-ship potential. The aircraft is seen here with a pair of Kormoran ASM on underfuselage stations, two AIM9s on the inboard stub pylons, two of the smaller GR1 type fuel tanks on the inboard wing stations and the outboard wing stations have been activated to carry Sky Shadow ECM pods. (BAe)

A pair of F3s taxi past a 101 Squadron VC10K2. (Hugh Harkins)

# 4

# Tornado F3 on Exercise

The skills of the Tornado F3 force are tested on a regular basis as much of the squadron's time is taken up preparing for and participating in various air defence exercises around the world. In the UK the two main exercises are Elder Forest and Elder Joust, the former is the larger of the two and is held annually in the spring. The basic scenario of the exercise has changed little with the thawing of east-west relations and the break up of the former Soviet Union. The RAF still trains to meet the formations of hostile strike aircraft and fighters that may be deployed against this island if the cold war flares up again.

During the exercise the defending fighters of 11 Group, the Tornado F3 Squadrons and the Hawk T1A trainers that would form part of the MFF in wartime, are deployed against a large force of enemy aircraft flying from bases in Denmark, Germany, France and, of course, the UK itself. These consist of Tornado GR1s, Jaguars, Harriers and Canberras of 360 ECM Squadron of the RAF, along with Tornados, Mirage 2000s, Mirage IVs, F16s and F15s from other NATO countries and France. Backing up the fighters of 11 Group are the E3D Sentries AWAC's aircraft from 8 Squadron Waddington, along with the vital VC10 and, to a lesser degree, Tristar tankers which are in a sense force multipliers as they allow the F3s to remain on CAP station for considerable periods of time.

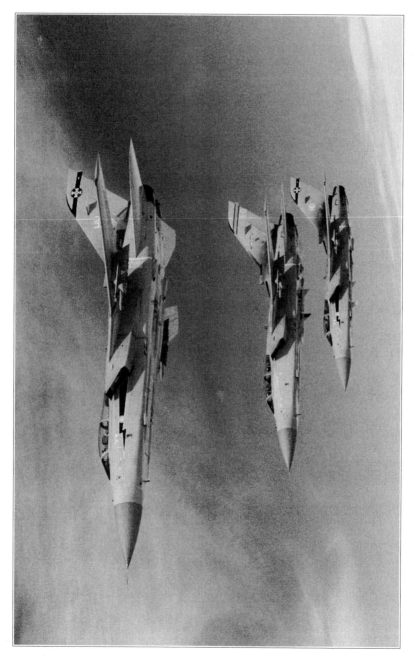

A pair of 111 Tremblers Squadron F3s flank a single 25 Squadron aircraft. The two furthest away aircraft each have a single Skyflash missile. (BAe)

ZE 202 AH 65R Squadron landing at Akrotiri, Cyprus. (BAe)

Incoming strike packages are located by E3D Sentry AWAC aircraft and the relevant information is then transferred by computer to H.Q. Strike Command at High Wycombe and other important radar stations such as Buchan and Boulmer.

The 1992 Elder Forest was held between 5 and 13 March. For the first time this exercise was linked with a naval exercise, namely Teamwork 92. This brought the air wings of the carriers *Invincible* with her Sea Harriers and the USS *Eisenhower* with her large complement of Tomcats, Hornets and Avengers. These two carriers were part of the Grey enemy force off the coast of Northern Scotland, with the Tomcats and Hornets providing the defending fighters with a somewhat different adversary to that normally encountered in such exercises.

The main enemy force, the Brown force, operated from NATO bases on the continent as well as some RAF stations, deploying various types of aircraft as mentioned above. In the past however, aircraft such as the F16 have had to simulate being Mig 29 Fulcrums but with the threat from the east relaxed they are now simply F16s as this type of aircraft can be expected to be encountered on some potential out of area hot spots.

The defending forces consisted of the seven Tornado F3 Squadrons, the two remaining Phantom FGR2 Squadrons (now retired) and the Hawk T1As of the reserve Squadrons along with the E3D Sentries of 8 Squadron. The enemy also had AWACS support in the shape of E3Fs of the Armée de l'Air.

The first part of the exercise was the normal probing flights by enemy MR aircraft before the massed air attacks started on 10 March to 13 March. Both attacking and defending forces get vast amounts of experience from the Forest series of exercise, and to answer the critics who question the need for such a large exercise now that the Soviet threat has diminished, it should be pointed

ZE 819 launches a Skyflash missile during a missile practice. (BAe)

Tornado F3, 29 Squadron, "Exercise Golden Eagle", Bridge over the River Kwai. (BAe)

out that the lessons learned and experience gained can be used in any theatre in which the RAF's fighters are deployed.

In accordance with the five nation defence agreement of 1971 signed by Britain, Australia, New Zealand, Malaysia and Singapore, the U.K. is committed to the defence of Malaysia and Singapore from outside threats. Since signing the agreement the U.K. has expended little energy in exercising its commitment, that is until the late 1980s. Since then the RAF has sent regular mixed detachments to the Far East to participate in air defence exercises.

Between 13 and 16 March 1988, 4 Tornado F3s belonging to No. 5 Squadron along with a pair of GR1s from 27 Squadron, supported by two VC10 K2s, took part in AIREX 90–2, an air defence exercise in Malaysia and Singapore. The role of the F3s was interception of incoming strike packages, they were vectored onto incoming aircraft by the local fighter controllers at the Integrated Air Defence System H.Q. located at Butterworth.

This was followed in 1989 by aircraft of 29 Squadron which participated in exercise Lima Bartistu while on a round the world deployment.

During ADEX 90–2 No 5 Squadron deployed four Tornado F3s, ZE762 CA, ZE737 CE, ZE734 CJ, and ZE738 CK to RMAF base Butterworth alongside a pair of 27 Squadron Tornado GR1s, ZD811 JY and ZD847 JZ. Supporting the aircraft were two 101 Squadron VC10 K2/3s, ZA143 D and ZA144 E and a Type 99 mobile radar captured from the Argentinians in 1982. The radar and other equipment as well as 260 personnel were transported from the UK in Tristar and Hercules transport aircraft. The operation was under the overall command of G/C Phil Roser.

The Tornado F3s were based in the four alert sheds at the end of Butterworth's main runway. The Tornado F3s were teamed with F5Es as part of the Defending force, pitted against them was a mixed bag of aircraft including the two 27 Squadron Tornado GR1s, six RAAF FA18 Hornets and six RAAF F111 strike aircraft, operating out of Williamstown air base. The attack was to be from a chain of fictitious islands in the South China Sea.

During the make-believe war attacking forces mounted about 140 sorties a day for the first three days, followed by 90 sorties on the fourth day, 16 March, for a total of 522 offensive sorties. Among the targets were the all important aerodromes, radar facilities and supply dumps. The aircraft of the IADS including the Tornado F MK3 were vectored onto incoming strike packages of up to 40 aircraft at a time. Due to the controllers being unused to such sophisticated interceptors as the Tornado F3 the RAF detachment was unable to operate to its full potential; perhaps therefore, in future exercises it would be beneficial for the RAF to deploy a pair of E3D sentries.

Six Tornado F3s along with four Harrier GR7s deployed to Malaysia towards the end of 1992. The six F3s were from 23 Squadron RAF Leeming and included ZE969 EA, ZE936 EE. The whole detachment was commanded by G/C David Henchen, G/C Air Defence HQ, Strike Command, High Wycombe. Both the Tornados and Harriers operated out of RMAF base Kuantan. Other British air defence elements consisted of the carrier HMS *Invincible* with its complement of Sea Harrier FRS1s, type 42 Destroyers, HMS *Newcastle* and HMS *Edinburgh*, all three vessels with Sea Dart SAMs were supported by RFA *Olwyn* and *Fort Austin*.

The RAF participated in its first Distant Frontier exercise, also the first North American exercise for the Tornado F3, during April 1992. Included in the RAF's contribution to the exercise were six Tornado GR MK1, two Tornado GR1As, an E3D sentry,

AEW MK1, and a VC10 K MK3 ZA149. Additionally a pair of Tristar tankers were used to trail the F3s and the two GR1As across the Atlantic.

At 11:05 on the morning of Monday 6 April four Tornado F3s ZE203, ZE210, ZE808 and ZE961, all to the latest Stage 1+ standard and all borrowed from 23 and 25 Squadrons of the Leeming wing, departed RAF Leuchars for Alaska. Approximately half an hour later a further two Tornados, ZE206 and ZE936, took off to join a pair of Tornado GR1As from II Squadron RAF Marham on the long transit to Goose Bay where the aircraft would stop over. With the distance involved the Tornados were assisted in their deployment by air-to-air refuelling by Tristar K MK1 ZD949 in the case of the first four, and KC MK1 ZD953 for the second pair of F3s, together with the GR1As. The second leg of the journey was from Goose Bay, Canada, to Eilson AFB, Alaska, and as this leg was longer than the first each Tristar took with it only three aircraft, thus the two GR1As were left behind at Goose Bay until they left for Eilson a few days later, in company with six GR1s from the RAF detachment Goose Bay. All six of the Tornado F3s arrived as scheduled in what was considered a combat capable condition at Eilson AFB on 8 April where they were greeted by some very harsh winter weather, a far cry from even the worst British winters.

The exercise was arranged into two phases, each of two weeks duration. The first phase was crewed by 111 Squadron F3s and 2 Squadron GR1/As, while 43 and 20 Squadrons respectively took over for the second fortnight. The F3s mainly put up four ship formations and during the first week flew against each other as well as some DACT with the American F16Cs in which the F3s did well using the F3's BVR capability to its advantage.

From the second week mixed packages were flown with F3s flying alongside F16Cs with USAF F15s acting as the enemy. At the start of any aerial engagement the Tornado F3s were usually outnumbered by the F15s; the supporting F16s lacked any BVR capability therefore were ineffective in air-to-air combat until the fighting got close. Despite these disadvantages the F3s performed extremely well against the supposedly superior F15s. While at the end of the day it was decided that honours were even, some were of the opinion that the F3s may just have got the better of the BVR engagements. Throughout the exercise the aircraft packages got larger until on the last day they peaked at a 28 aircraft package.

The main objective of the Tornado F3 detachment was to give the crews a measure of experience in operating four ship formations in the sweep role, sanitising the sky ahead of a strike package of GR1/As and F16s, as opposed to the interception role performed daily in the UK. The main benefits of operating in Alaska were the unrestricted air space and sparse population, thus allowing aircraft to fly faster and lower than is possible in the UK. Also it gave the ground crews invaluable experience in servicing and maintaining the fighters while 8000 miles from base with limited spares back-up and in an environment that frequently had blizzards and temperatures well below −20°.

In May 1993 aircraft and crews from the Leuchars Wing once again went to Alaska at the invitation of the Americans hoping to expand on their successes of 1992.

The Tornado F3 made its debut at Nellis for Red Flag 93–1. A total of six aircraft, ZE763 BA in the markings of 29 Squadron Coningsby, ZE887 DJ and ZE982 DM 11 Squadron Leeming, ZE807 EN 23 Squadron Leeming, ZE902 FJ 25 Squadron Leeming. All except ZE763 were to Stage 1+ standard with RAM on the wing and fin leading edges. Three squadrons 5, 11, and 29

As part of the RAF's mixed fighter force Tornados regularly train with BAe Hawks TIAs of the reserve squadrons. (BAe)

At the end of each sortie the aircraft are returned to their HAS. Here is an aircraft in the process of being winched backwards to its shelter. (Hugh Harkins)

each participated for a two week period, all using the same aircraft. The F3s were supported throughout the exercise period by two Victor K2 tankers that were to refuel the F3s on the Northern edge of the range area before they were committed to battle.

The main task of the Tornado F3s during Red Flag was to provide fighter sweep escorts for the strike packages including Tornado GR1s with four ships of F3s sanitising the sky ahead of the strike aircraft. Red Flag gave F3 crews a chance to practise counter air sorties. Each pilot was allowed to fly only once a day due to the extensive briefing and debriefing required to maximise each sortie. Two waves of aircraft were flown each day, at 13.00 hours for day operations and 18.00 hours for night missions. Crews were to fly one week on night sorties and one on day sorties.

While the regular series of home and foreign based air defence exercises gives the crews the opportunity to practise and develop tactics that can and would be employed in war situations, it is at Missile Practice Camp that they actually get to fire a live air-to-air missile.

The RAF interceptor Squadrons regularly deploy to RAF Valley, Wales, for Missile Practice Camp (MPC) where chosen crews get to fire at least one air-to-air missile at a towed target. The Strike Command Air to Air Missile Establishment (STCAAME) is the unit responsible for all aspects of these deployments. Before this unit came into being the job was the responsibility of Fairey Aviation using Supermarine Swift fighters armed with Firefly missiles; later Fighter Command took over the role, flying a mixture of Swift, Gloucester, Javelin and BAC Lightning fighters armed with Red Top and Firestreak missiles. The unit can only carry out live missile firings in conjunction with RAE facilities at RAE Llanbedr and RAE Aberporth. Aberporth has full operational control over the range area in Cardigan Bay where most of the

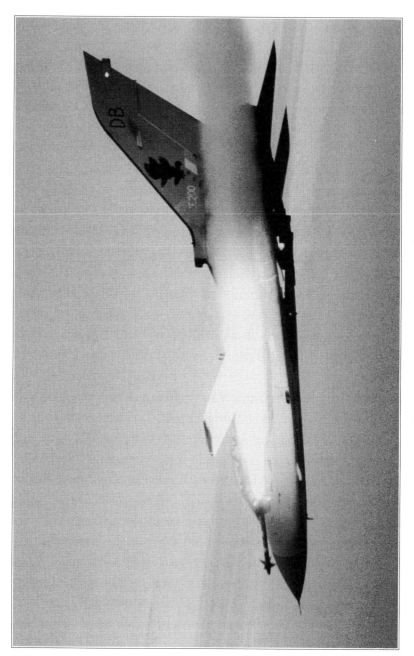

ZE 200 launching a Sidewinder. (BAe)

missile firings take place. Llanbedr provides the targets in the shape of Jindivik MK103B pilotless drones. The drones are controlled remotely from Llanbedr although directions come from Aberporth. Confusingly the Jindivik drone is not the actual target but instead acts as a target tower towing targets at various distances from the drone.

The second target type is the Stiletto high speed target whose two fuel rocket motors give it a speed of Mach 0.95 at low level and Mach 2 at altitudes in excess of 50,000ft.

Normally the missile firing is separated into three categories: the first and most realistic from the crew's point of view is the no-notice scramble of Tornado F3s on Quick Reaction Alert (QRA); this is possible as these aircraft are fully armed and ready to meet any intruder straying into the UK; the second category is the short notice exercise launches; last is the planned MPC. This last category normally uses missiles which have been fitted with instrumentation transmitters.

The first category, the QRA launch, is primarily to test the combat readiness of the fighting Squadron aircraft weapons and crew. The aircraft would be launched in the normal QRA manner from its home base, most likely RAF Leuchars, only once they are airborne will the crew know what is happening. After the missile firing the Tornado will recover to Valley where the crew will undergo a debrief. By far the most complex category is the MPC, these detachments usually of about six aircraft crews and ground support, are planned well in advance.

Once a squadron leaves Valley at the end of its camp the work is just beginning for the Engineering Analysis Report Progression and Statistics team (EARPS) which is a part of STCAAME. This unit examines the films of firings from the chase planes and firing aircraft if fitted. The telemetry records produced by RAE

Aberporth are analyzed along with the radar tracking and missile-miss distance measurements.

Unfortunately the MPC does not allow all crews to fire missiles, not least due to the expense of each missile. For the lucky crews who do fire a missile the experience gained is invaluable. Perhaps the STCAAME motto sums up the necessity of the MPC: *By practice we validate.*

Immediately before, during, and after the Gulf War of 1991 the STCAAME saw a large increase in business. Jaguars, Buccaneers Tornado GR1s, and of course Tornado F3 units, all competed for available range time in order to bring aircraft and crews up to a war footing to enable them to meet any air-to-air opposition that the Iraqi AF might offer. In the end, and much to the dismay of the fighter crews, the Iraqis opted not to fight.

ZE 811 HB of 111 Squadron launches at the beginning of an Elder Joust 93 sortie. (Hugh Harkins)

ZE758C of 1435 Flt. outside its hangar at Mount Pleasant airbase, Falkland Islands. The aircraft is armed with four winders and only two Skyflash which is the standard armament for Falklands operations. (RAF Strike Command, via author).

# 5

# Tornado at War – Desert Shield/Storm and Operation Deny Flight

The Tornado F3 was one of the first aircraft to be sent to Saudi Arabia following the Iraqi invasion of Kuwait on 2 August 1990. On 9 August the government announced plans to send a force of aircraft to help deter further Iraqi aggression against Saudi Arabia where its armies were now massing. A force of Tornado F3s was already in the Mediterranean as 11 F3s of No 29 Squadron were on APC at RAF Akrotiri Cyprus. Six of these aircraft, ZE289 BA, ZE338 BB, ZE258 BE, ZE254 BG, ZE255 BH and ZE205 BF, were flown out to Dhahran on 10 August where they were joined on the 12th by a further six: ZE762 CA, ZE758 CB, ZE163 CF, ZE732 CH, ZE734 CJ and ZE736 CK from No 5 Squadron flown out from RAF Coningsby. The Tornados were based alongside No 29 Squadron RSAF, also equipped with Tornado F3s. Five of No 5 Squadron's aircraft also joined the five remaining No 29 Squadron Tornados on Cyprus where they stayed until relieved by six Phantoms from No 19 Squadron Wildenrath. Protection for the Tornados and other aircraft based at Dhahran was provided by the BAe Rapier SAMs of No 20 Squadron RAF Regiment which arrived in Saudi Arabia during 11–12 August, but as there was sufficient protection at the base they were re-directed to Muharaq Bahrain.

Both half squadrons were formed into No 5 composite Squadron under the command of W/C Euan Black. No 5C Squadron and the Saudis worked closely together, flying CAPs along the Saudi Kuwait Iraq border. As it had been flown out at short notice it was decided to replace 5 Composite Squadron with another unit which would be equipped with modified Tornados, mostly taken from the Leuchars wing from where they had just been delivered. The changeover began on 29 August when eight aircraft, ZE961 DH flown by W/C Hamilton, ZE203 DA, ZE208 DC, ZE210 DD, ZE936 DF, ZE962 DI, ZE968 DJ and ZE934 DV were flown out to Cyprus. Six of these flew on to Dhahran the following day allowing six 5 Squadron aircraft to return home. The following week saw a further six modified aircraft installed at Dhahran.

Most of the new Tornados were from Block 13 ZE859 onwards and so were to the latest Stage 1 standard with Stage 1 AA AI.24 Foxhunter radar. These aircraft had only just been delivered to the Leuchars wing from BAe Warton for the formation of No. 111 Squadron. The whole RAF F3 fleet has since been upgraded to at least Stage 1 standard.

For service in the Gulf region some Tornado F3s were further Upgraded to Stage 1+. Included in the Stage 1+ upgrade was the addition of improved cooling and revised software for the Foxhunter, including ECM and close combat capability, and an F/A18 type combat stick top which contains all the buttons and switches needed for close combat engagements, this speeds up the pilot's reaction time to a threat. The existing Marconi Hermes Radar Homing and Warning Receiver (RHWR) has also been further improved. Another important feature of the upgrade was the addition of an emergency power boost switch by the throttle which can give an extra 5% power to each engine if required. The standard MK104 is rated at 9,105lbst dry and 16,523lbst with

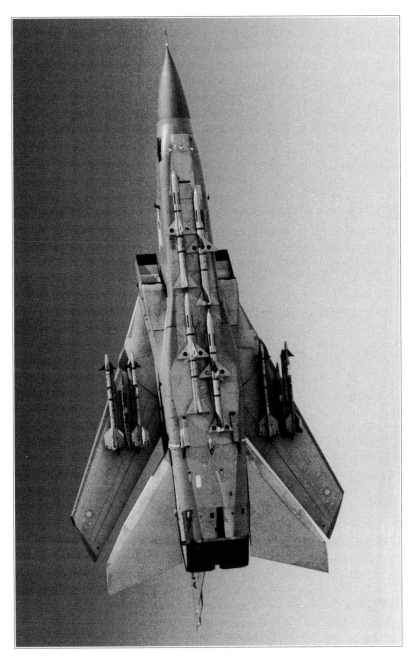

A fully armed F3 with wings in the 67° position. (BAe)

reheat, the modifications ups this to by 5% by allowing the stator temperature to increase by 20°C from 1,290°–1,310°. The drawback of this is a shorter time between overhauls.

The F3s were modified to enable them to use NVGs, experience of which had been gained by the F3 Operational Evaluation Unit at Coningsby. New tactics were developed for the use of NVGs after which all F3 crews underwent a night work-up phase to familiarise themselves with their use. Another addition not normally worn in peacetime was the AR5 respirator which is worn in flight, protecting the crews from chemical attack.

On the defensive side of the upgrade was the fitting of two tracer AN/ALE–40 (V) flare dispensers underneath the rear fuselage on the engine access doors. Each dispenser contains fifteen compartments. The flare dispensers protect the aircraft against heat seeking missiles but for protection against radar guided missiles a Philips-Matra Phimat chaff pod was carried on the port wing pylon instead of a drop tank. The second drop tank was reinstated when the pod was relocated.

For operations in the hot climate the Tornados had their air conditioning systems uprated and the cockpit canopies were modified to prevent heat buckling, a problem that had plagued the original deployment; in addition new tyres were introduced for use in the hot climate. Although the original Tornado deployment had used the standard AIM9L a special purchase from the US of the improved AIM9M for the Tornado has improved the close combat capabilities still further. The 9 Mike has an improved seeker head, the WGU–4A/B and the MK36 mod 11 rocket motor.

Most visible of the changes has been the addition of Radar Absorbent Material (RAM) to the leading edges of the fin from the air scoop to the black dialectic panel at the tip, and the wing leading edges, apart from the dialectic panels for the RWR on the non moving inboard part.

On 14 September it was announced that a further six F3s, ZE203 DA, ZE907 DK, ZE159 DO, ZE165 DU, ZE941 DW and ZE963 DX would be sent to Dhahran to reinforce the squadron already there. These arrived at the base on 22 September. On 1 December the Tornado F3 detachment was taken over by personnel from No. 43 Squadron Leuchars and No. 29 Squadron Coningsby being formed into No. 43 composite Squadron with W/C Andy Moir in overall command. The squadron had been notified only on the 29 November and within 48 hours was installed at Dhahran. On 2 December the new unit began flying CAPs in rotation with Saudi and USAF Tornado F3s and F15 Eagles. Between then and the 15 January deadline the F3 crews were busy flying CAPs and dissimilar air combat training sorties against such types as Mirage F1s, Tornado GR1, Jaguars and FA/A18 Hornets.

Just prior to the beginning of offensive operations on 17 January the F3 squadron operation was moved to the protection of an underground bunker, at the same time the aircraft were given additional protection in the shape of splinter shields.

As the hours ticked away to the beginning of Desert Storm the squadron received the order to implement the offensive liberation of Kuwait, code word WOLFPACK, with H hour at 0300 local on the morning of 17 January.

When war finally came in the early hours of 17 January the Tornado F3s were tasked with protecting Saudi territory from Iraqi bombers and with flying escort sorties for tankers and E3A AWACS aircraft. For this they were in standard war fit, armed with four underfuselage Skyflash BVR missiles, three AIM9M Sidewinder short range air to air missiles and a single 27mm

Mouser cannon. The fourth 'winder rail was occupied by a Phimat chaff dispenser. The F3s each carried two of the large 2250ltr drop tanks and had their already impressive CAP radius extended further by use of inflight refuelling, normally from Tristar K MK1s.

On 18 January two F3s on CAP, one of which had W/C Andy Moir OC No. 43 Squadron at the controls, committed north into Kuwait. They had been tasked to help a formation of USAF A10 ground attack aircraft which were escaping south, pursued by a pair of Iraqi AF fighters which turned out to be Mirage F1s. Once alerted the F3s accelerated and blew off their Hindenburger wing tanks in order to make their mounts more manoeuvrable. Once they had detected their targets the F3s locked them up from long range with their Foxhunter AI24 radar. The Iraqis, after probably being alerted of the Tornados' presence by their RWRs, elected not to fight, instead turning and running away north.

On 18 February a pair of 43 Tornados were vectored north by AWACS to intercept a pair of enemy aircraft that had been detected flying south fast at medium altitude. By the time the F3s had closed to within 10nm of the targets they had disappeared from AWACS radar, although the F3 still had radar returns on their Foxhunter sets of the last known position of the contacts these looked more like chaff than actual aircraft. Moments later another pair of aircraft were detected and the F3s headed for them but these turned out to be a pair of F4G Phantoms. Both formations acknowledged each other's presence with the old fashioned wing rock, and with the excitement over, the Tornados headed back to Saudi territory over 150 miles distant. The return flight was far from boring as the RHWR constantly alerted the F3 crews that enemy radar was tracking them.

This incident was one of only a few occasions that the F3s confronted enemy aircraft, indeed the main threat turned out to be from SAM and AAA once the F3s moved north to patrol over Kuwait. The fighters were briefed to avoid the main zones protected by the large SAMs and flew above the ceiling of the smaller SAMs and most of the AAA.

Just before the start of the ground war the F3s CAP stations were pulled back behind the allied lines, allowing the artillery to fire at targets in Iraq without fear of hitting friendly aircraft on CAP.

Night sorties were a common practice for the F3 detachment, this required great skill from the crews as aircraft had to fly with lights out for obvious reasons. As previously mentioned, the interceptor crews were well versed in the use of night vision goggles. It was during a night sortie that a pair of Tornados flying CAP on the Saudi Kuwait Iraq border were ordered to proceed some 60 miles into Iraq. As there was no mention of enemy aircraft the F3 crews enquired as to why. They were told that they were to assist in the search for a downed allied aircraft as their NVGs were excellent for this purpose. AWACS had passed the coded frequency to the F3s coded Bentley in order for them to try and contact the downed aircraft. This was to no avail, therefore Bentley 01 dropped down to low level in the hope of locating them visually while Bentley 02 remained at medium altitude to provide cover against any Iraqi aerial threat.

After some 40 minutes on station lack of fuel dictated that Bentley leave the area, leaving the search operation in the hands of AWACS and other allied aircraft in the vicinity.

As the war progressed the F3 began flying CAPs over Kuwait and Iraq. For all the squadron's efforts no kills were made. This was by no means the fault of the squadron, rather the opposite, as the Iraq Air Force opted not to fight and instead hid in Iran. Even so most of the USAF kills were against aircraft fleeing to Iran. With the end of hostilities the squadron continued flying

With the beginning of the ground war the F3s moved their CAPs over Kuwait itself; here ZE200 W is flying over the burning oil wells. (Crown Copyright)

CAPs until 8 March when it was stood down. The unit was returned to RAF Leuchars and Coningsby on 13 March 1991.

At about 11.00hrs on the morning of 13 March 1991, three separate pairs of Tornado F MK3s performed two low level passes over RAF Coningsby, followed by a six ship formation fly-past, before breaking into the circuit to land. The six aircraft were, ZE763 BA, ZE887 E, ZE160 Z, ZE20? B, ZE941 R and ZE961 H. One of the aircraft, ZE763, which was flown by W/C Roy Trotter, CO of No. 29 Squadron was decorated in full squadron markings of XXX on the engine intakes and the Eagle/Buzzard badge on the fin. All six aircraft were equipped with a full war fit of four Skyflash and three AIM9M Sidewinder AAMs; the fourth sidewinder station, the starboard outer, was occupied by a Phimat chaff dispenser. All aircraft carried the 2250 litre (495imp gal) drop tanks.

On 25 February 1992 four RAF F3s and a VC10 tanker took part in a fly-past over Kuwait City, marking the Kuwait national day and the first anniversary of the cease fire. As part of the UK's commitment to the Gulf region a detachment of six Tornado F3s from No. 43 Squadron, Leuchars, went to Kuwait to participate in exercise Free Sky in November 1992. While in the Gulf the F3s participated in exercises with the USN.

The Tornado F3s' next operational deployment was to help enforce the UN Air Exclusion Zone (AEZ) over Bosnia Hercigovina. Six Tornado F3s, including ZE936 EE, ZE961 FD, ZE164 DA and ZE210 FB from No. 23 Squadron at RAF Leeming were sent to Italy on 18 April 1993, and a further two on May 13. Staffing the squadron on the ground and in the air were 20 aircrew and 167 ground crew.

The first sorties took place on the 26th. The first attempted interception of a violating aircraft was on 29 April when two

As well as RAF F3s the 24 Saudi aircraft were employed on CAPs. (BAe)

Tornados were vectored towards a contact which was lost before the fighters could visually identify it. The UN AEZ was authorized on 15 September 1992, but as no hardware was provided to enforce it the warring factions were able to defy it as and when they desired. Between September 1992 and the middle of 1993 over 500 violations had been recorded. The UN asked NATO to enforce the AEZ in December 1992 but this was refused after a vote of 13–3. On the other hand NATO voted to enforce it if the UN issued a resolution authorising its enforcement. By January 1993 the Serbs were on full alert against possible NATO air strikes. On 31 March 1993 the UN passed a resolution to allow the AEZ to be enforced, this was to start from 7 April 1993. The rules of engagement are still not fully public but it is understood that pilots must repeatedly warn the violating aircraft. After the UN's decision to enforce the zone the NATO forces tasked with the enforcement began to assemble at bases in Italy and aboard carriers in the Adriatic. These included 12 F15Cs at Aviano, 12 FA18As on the carrier *Theodore Roosevelt*, 18 Dutch F16As, 10 Mirage 2000Cs and 4 Mirage F1Cs from France at Cervia, Turkey, 18 F16As to Ghedi and Britain, 8 Tornado F3s from Leeming deployed to Gioia del Colle.

The Tornado used to enforce the AEZ are all to Stage 1 + standard with the same mods as incorporated for the Gulf War. One of the few changes has been to the weapons load carried whereas in the Gulf the F3s had one AIM9M deleted to make room for a Phimat chaff dispenser, over Bosnia the aircraft carry two Phimat pods and only two winders, the pods being on the outer pylons of the fuel tanks. On 13 May two F3 were sent to investigate a Croatian Mil Mi 8 Hip transport helicopter and subsequently forced it to land. After landing the aircraft, supposedly on a cas. evac. mission, was found to be carrying 20,000 rounds of ammunition.

For patrols over Bosnia two CAP stations have been established: the first in the north covers Banja Luka/Tuzla and their surrounding areas, the other in the South covers the Mostar Sarajevo area. Inflight refuelling is required to keep the fighters on station in the CAP areas, for this reason a 24 hour tanker track has been established near the Croatian city of Split. A typical fighter sortie lasts four to five hours. All UN fighters fly in pairs, usually in a race track pattern, over the designated CAP station, here they wait for the AWACS to call them to investigate suspected violations.

By 15 May 22 probable and 4 confirmed violations had been detected, this had risen to 10 confirmed by the end of the month.

Two VC10 K2/3s deployed to Sigonolla but were later moved to Milan-Malpensa, their task is to provide inflight refuelling for RAF and other NATO fighters. The VC10 detachment flew its first Deny Flight supporting sorties on 22 April. The VC10s were replaced by Tristar K1s after flying 45 sorties.

In Operation Grapple during May 1993 Tornado F3s and RN Sea King HC 4s were pitted against each other during a fighter evasion exercise over the hills and valleys of Wales, specifically the low flying area around Llanidloes.

The exercise involved two separate pairs of F3s, one each from No. 23 and No. 25 Squadrons RAF Leeming, the F3s were supported by an E3D Sentry AEW MK1 as they are over Bosnia. The targets for the fighters were three Sea King HC4s from 845 and 846 NAS, with the one from No. 845 Squadron painted overall white for UN operations in the former Yugoslavia.

The operation began at 12.30 with all three helicopters with the call sign Yankee flying in loose tactical formation to allow the best chance of escape manoeuvres if attacked. The helicopters were flying at heights of around 100ft (30m), and with the threat of air attack looming, flew the aircraft between valleys rather than over and avoided overflying the many lakes in the area as this is a dead give away to high flying fighters.

Once the Sentry has located the helicopters it alerts the fighters and vectors them towards the targets. Once in the general area the fighters can either use their own Foxhunter radar or use the MK1 eyeball to locate and attack them visually. It is reported the F3 crews are now confident in their radar's ability to pick up a Sea King sized target flying at a height of less than 100ft (30m). Both pairs of Tornado F3s, 23 Squadrons call sign Javelin and 25 Squadron's call sign Jacket, were able to practise several interceptions, mainly 27mm cannon attacks using both radars and visually identification procedures. Once located the fighters would either attack in pairs or one at a time, with one aircraft flying high and the other trying to force the elusive helicopters out into the open ground. The F3s did not have it all their own way and several times darted up and down the target area before finding their targets.

During the exercise a strict set of rules of engagement were in force, the helicopters were to stay below 250ft while the F3s were to stay above that altitude, therefore the F3s were not to attack the helicopters from underneath. This exercise once again demonstrated that the F3 is no slouch in aerial combat, even against highly manoeuvrable helicopters with the fighters involved in some extremely tight turns thus leaving the defending helicopters little time to head for cover before the next attack was started.

The exercise was curtailed after one hour, but was considered a success giving the Tornados and Sea King crews valuable experience in fighter v helicopter combats. It must be hoped that these types of training sorties become more common in order to give crews of both types invaluable experience for future UN roles, such as that seen in Bosnia today.

During the first month of operation Deny Flight UN fighters had flown 1,022 sorties from 12 April to 11 May. Of this the RAF's Tornado F3s had flown 55 sorties while the supporting VC10s had totalled 20 sorties. By February 2 1994 this total had risen to 810 missions for the Tornado F3s.

Throughout 1993 the three squadrons of the Leeming wing contributed aircraft and crews to the detachment which was then taken over by the Coningsby wing on 25 November starting with No. 5 Squadron, followed by No. 29 Squadron in March 1994. The two squadrons of the Leuchars wing then took over the detachment starting with No. 43 Squadron in May followed by No. 111 Squadron. Normal F3 CAP sorties are in the region of three hours although missions of up to six and a half hours have been recorded.

Events in Bosnia took a new turn on 28 February when a pair of USAF F16C on CAP intercepted and shot down four out of a strike package of six Serbian Soko Super Galeb ground attack aircraft which were clearly violating the UN enforced No Fly Zone. This event will go down in history as being the first time NATO forces have fired a shot in anger since its conception in 1949. Following on from this first air-to-air action a pair of USAF F16C Falcons bombed a Serb command post at 16.29 GMT on 10 April in an attempt to halt the assault on the UN designated safe haven of Gorazde; this attack was guided by an SAS patrol on the ground. The following day a pair of USMC FA18C Hornets bombed and fired 20mm cannon at a group of vehicles, destroying on tank, three APCs and a lorry. On the 15th a French Navy Etendard IVP was hit by ground fire while conducting a recon-naissance over Gorazde but managed to make it back to its carrier,

*Clemencheu.* On the 16th the RN lost a Sea Harrier FRS1 which was shot down most probably by a SA7 Grail SAM while conducting a recce over Gorazde. By 27 April the Serbs had pulled their heavy weapons back 20km from the town to comply with the UN demands, although by that time the Serbs had achieved most of their objectives.

After this things generally quietened down until 5 August when Serb forces snatched a T55 tank two APCs and AAA guns from UN storage near Sarajevo. A French Puma that gave chase was hit by small arms, fired and broke off the chase. In response to this the UN launched a total of four French Mirage F1CTs from Istrana, Four Jaguar GR1As from Gio del Colle, four Dutch F16As from Aviano. Of this impressive strike force only the A10s attacked, firing about 600 rounds of 30mm cannon destroying a Serb M-18 tank destroyer; the other aircraft were unable to attack due to either bad weather or the fact that they could not locate ground targets. Following this NATO launched a retaliatory strike in response to an attack on UN forces in Sarajevo. This air attack took place near the village of Osijerk, 6km from Sarajevo, and involved an USAF A10A which strafed a T55 tank with 30mm cannon fire, following which two RAF Jaguar GR1As each dropped a single 1000lb bomb on the target.

By mid November Croatian Serb forces were threatening the UN designated Safe Haven of Bihac in Northern Bosnia; they further challenged the UN by flying bombing raids on Bihac from the Krajina Serb held Croatian airfield of Udbina. The first raid on 18 November consisted of a pair of J-22 Orao fighter bombers which bombed positions inside the UN designated safe area of Bihac. The following day a further pair of J-22 Orao bombed the ammunition factory at Cazin about 10 miles (16km) to the North of Bihac. On this raid one of the aircraft crashed after hitting the

With the war over 43 Squadron returned to RAF Leuchars on 13.3.91.
Here ZE966 is saluted by a Wessex HC2 of resident 22 B flight 22 Squadron. (Crown Copyright)

chimney of a building during its approach to the target. In response to this the UN mounted the largest air strike yet, at 10.30 am GMT on 21 November with about 30 aircraft, including two RAF Jaguar GR1s and two FAA Sea Harrier FRS1s together with USMC FA18Ds of VMFA332, F15Es 48th FW, F16Cs 31st FW, EF111As 27th FW, Dutch F16As 1st FW and French Jaguars EC11, Mirage 2000Cs EC5 and Mirage F1CRs EC30 involved. The target was the Serb held airfield at Udbina. The raid was a total success with direct hits on the single runway and Serb claims that up to 20 fixed wing aircraft were destroyed on the ground, although official policy was not to target any ground based aircraft.

The following day a pair of RN Sea Harriers on recce North of Bihac were fired on by a pair of SA2 SAMs which missed by about 2 miles, exploding at an altitude of 35,000 ft (10,668m). This was the second time Sea Harriers had been fired on near Bihac as a pair were fired on by SAMs on 8 September. To deter further action the UN mounted another strike of about 20 aircraft to destroy the SAM battery at Otoka, 15 miles (24km) North of Bihac on the 23rd. *En route* to the target the strike package was targeted by two other SA2 SAM sites at Basonka Krupa and Dvor in Serbia Krajina over the Croatian border, these sites were subsequently bombed in self defence by four F15Es of the 48FW. Post strike recce showed that the SAM site at Otoka had not been destroyed, although the radars had been hit the missiles were still intact. A further strike of 20 aircraft was launched later that day to finish the destruction. By the 25th, with mounting pressure to do something to help the refugees and stranded UN peacekeepers in Bihac, the UN finally asked NATO to provide close air support around Bihac; although a strike was launched no attacks were made, reportedly due to bad visibility in the target area. Tornado F3s along with other NATO fighters provided top cover for the attack aircraft. A further strike was planned for the 26th but was cancelled in order to give diplomacy a chance. Later on the 26th a pair of RAF Tornado F3s were fired on by a SAM, thought to be an SA6, over Dorni Vacuf. Neither of the aircraft was hit and both returned safely to Gio.

As this is written in November 1994 RAF Tornado F3s as well as the fighters of other NATO nations are still flying CAPS over Bosnia. Only time will tell if the Serbs will again challenge the technologically and numerically superior NATO air force facing them, and if so will NATO and the UN put aside the political differences and finally respond in force. If not then perhaps the time will have come for the UN to pull out of Bosnia altogether and lift the arms embargo.

# 6

# RAF Leuchars
# Front Line Fighter Station

Royal Air Force Leuchars is the oldest military airbase still operational in Scotland. The station is located south of Dundee about three miles from St Andrews, Fife. Leuchars, Britain's premier fighter station, has an establishment of two squadrons of Tornado F3s, 43F and 111F Squadrons, and directly employs 2000 service and civilian personnel.

Leuchars' association with aviation began 82 years ago when the Army flew balloons from the site. Later, during and after World War I, the Royal Navy operated training aircraft from the base. In 1920 the RAF moved in, sharing the station with the senior service until 1936 when the station was turned over to RAF Coastal Command who flew an assortment of types from here during and after World War II.

In September 1950 RAF Fighter Command took over the running of Leuchars when Gloucester Meteor moved in; these were followed during the 50s and 60s by Javelins, Hunters and Lightnings. In 1968 No 43 Squadron, the Fighting Cocks, took up residence with Phantom FG1s. 43's Phantoms were to partner the Lightning F6s of 23 Squadron until Treble One (111F Squadron) moved North with its Phantom FGR2s in November 1975. 111F Squadron's FGR2s were replaced by de-navalised FG1s from

1978–80. During the 70s and 80s both squadrons were maintained at Leuchars with the FG1 covering the Northern QRA of the United Kingdom Air Defence Region (UKADR) which covers some 4,000,000 sq miles.

The Leuchars squadrons were the last to convert to the Tornado F3 after Coningsby and Leeming; the first to convert from the Phantom FG1 was 43 (F) Squadron which received its first two aircraft very publicly during the annual Battle of Britain airshow in September 1989. The squadron flew its last Phantom sortie on 31 December 1989. After working up 43 was declared operational on 1 July 1990, immediately being assigned to SACLANT for air defence of the U.K. as well as defence of the fleet.

On 2 August of that year Iraq invaded neighbouring Kuwait, an action which received worldwide condemnation and subsequently resulted in the assembling of a vast air, sea and ground force by the U.N. Coalition Forces. Whilst No 43 was not included in the original composite squadron detached to Dhahran, Saudi Arabia, it formed part of the second detachment along with personnel from No. 29 Squadron from early December onwards. Immediately on arrival the squadron began flying CAPs along the Saudi/Iraqi border in rotation with US and Saudi F15 Eagles and Saudi Tornado F3s. Once hostilities started the Tornados were assigned to fly defensive CAPs which eventually extended deep into Iraq. With the cease-fire in effect the squadron stopped operations on 3 March and returned to Leuchars on 13 March 1991.

111F Squadron was the last squadron to form on the F3, flying its last Phantom sortie on 30 January 1990. The unit's first Tornados arrived in May 1990, these aircraft were straight off the Warton production line and therefore to the latest Stage 1 standards. The RAF's commitment to the Gulf operations saw the squadron losing its new aircraft to the Leeming wing receiving older machines with stage Z radar in their place. The Squadron was officially declared to NATO SACUER on 1 January 1991 although with No. 43 Squadron deployed to the Gulf, 111 actually held the stations QRA commitment for a full month in December 1990.

More recently, on 6 April 1992, 111 Squadron deployed six aircraft borrowed from the Leeming Stage 1+ standard machines to Alaska for exercise Distant Frontier 92/1. This was the first time the RAF had deployed here for exercises with the USAF. After two weeks No 43 Squadron took over the detachment; both squadrons reportedly achieved the goals they had set, and with the tactics employed, did extremely well against USAF F15 Eagles. In May 1993, 43 Squadron deployed 6 Tornados to Gibraltar and 111 Squadron once more departed for Alaska to participate in the Distant Frontier 93/1 Exercise.

For training purposes the Tornados F3s from the Leuchars wing transit to an allocated area over the North Sea of the East coast of Southern Scotland where they perform practice interceptions against each other as well as Tornado F3s of other units. For dissimilar air combat training they can engage other types, such as Tornado GR1, Jaguar GR1 and Harrier GR7, which can prove to be tricky opponents in close combat, as can the Hawks of Nos 4 and 7 FTS. In times of tension or war the Hawks of the reserve squadrons would assume their wartime role of air defence, armed with a pair (which can be increased to four) of AIM9L Sidewinder air-to-air missiles.

In 1979 a decision was taken to arm the Hawk with a pair of AIM9L Sidewinder AAMs in order to give it a secondary war role of point defence of the UK's airfields. It had originally been hoped to form a third Lightning squadron but this idea was dropped in favour of the Hawk. The conversions were done under

ZE730 GL is launched on a Q alert on 16 September 1993; this was only the second alert in two years. (Hugh Harkins)

Later that day the same aircraft lands back at RAF Leuchars. (Hugh Harkins)

the name of the Hawk war role programme with the work being carried out by BAe. Work was started in early 1980 with the first Sidewinder firing in this year also. Due to some minor problems the 'winder Hawk combination was not cleared for use until May 1983. On 31 January an official contract for the conversion of 89 Hawk T MK1s to T MK1A standard was awarded to BAe. Included in the modifications was the fitting of a Ferranti F.195 weapon sight along with strobe lights and a twin gyro platform to provide a high altitude accuracy reference system. The aircraft selected for modification came from the two TWUs and the Central Flying School (CFS) at RAF Scampton. This latter unit included the Red Arrows who would form as a squadron in the event of war. The other units would be 19, 74, 92 and 208 Reserve Squadrons.

The last of the modified Hawks was delivered to the RAF in August 1986, by which time the operational role had changed from that of point defence of military installations to the more aggressive one of meeting the enemy as far from friendly shores as possible. As the Hawk has no radar of its own it would fly with Tornado F3s as part of a mixed fighter force. Typically a single Tornado would fly with a pair of Sidewinder armed Hawks. Once an incoming strike package had been detected by either E3D Sentry AWACS, a Type 42 AD Destroyer, or the Tornado's own Foxhunter radar the Tornado would set up an interception profile with its own radar. If the rules of engagement allowed it the Tornado would launch its Sky Flash Missiles from BVR in order to take out some of the enemy before the fighting came in close, after which it would close in on the enemy aircraft with the Hawks following. Where a fighter escort was present, the more agile Hawks would take them on, leaving the Tornados free to concentrate on the primary mission of destroying the bombers.

In the MFF the Hawk/Tornado combination has proved to be a workable success with the Hawk proving to be an extremely capable day fighter. Although the Hawk is slow subsonic compared with modern purpose designed fighters, such as the F15 Eagle, it does have a number of advantages such as its smoke free engine, small size and low radar signature, all of which make the aircraft hard to detect in combat. The Hawk has proved to be extremely agile with a manoeuvring limit of +9g/−3g and while on detachments to the Air Combat Manoeuvring Instrumentation (ACME) range at Deccimommannu is well used to winning its fight, be it against F16s, F15s or F/A18s, the so called crop of agile fighters.

During these training sorties the engagements could consist of relatively simple 1v1 1v2 before moving on to the more complicated 2v2 2v4 and so on. During practice intercepts they work closely with Ground Controlled Intercept personal (GCI) at RAF Buchan Sector Operations Centre (SOC) as well as RAF and NATO E3 Sentries. The information provided by Buchan or the E3D is intended to enable the Tornado to reach a position from which a kill can be achieved. Such data will include target altitude and bearing relative to the friendly, as well as course instructions to enable them to reach a point where a radar contact can be achieved. Once radar contact has been confirmed they are on their own to conduct the combat. The Tornados fight each other or other aircraft such as Tornado GR1s and Hawk T1s.

Both squadrons of the Leuchars fighter wing each have 11 Hardened Aircraft Shelters (HAS) with 43 Squadron to the north of runway 09/27 and 111 to the south. HAS provide the Tornado with protection against air attack and the squadrons operate directly from their respective shelter villages, thus ending the traditional flight line operations previously used. As the normal squadron complement is 15 aircraft each, (at the time of writing 111

With St Andrews bay as a backdrop ZH558 GF of 43 Squadron deploys its thrust reverse buckets while positioning for take-off during Elder Joust 93. (Hugh Harkins)

Photographed from an accompanying vehicle ZE837 HY is returning to 111's HAS complex. (Hugh Harkins)

The author in the cockpit of Tornado F3 ZE835 HK from 111 Squadron. The large object at the back is actually part of the ejection seat, the whole unit ejecting with its occupant in the event of an emergency. (Hugh Harkins)

Markings worn on the front fuselage of 111 aircraft are a black lightning flash with a yellow border. (Hugh Harkins)

While each squadron has a normal complement of between 13 and 15 aircraft each they have only 11 HAS. To compensate for this the F3 Squadron have the Phase Three HAS which can house 2 aircraft in staggered formation. (Hugh Harkins)

Squadron having a complement of 18), it is routine for some aircraft to double up in the one shelter. For this they are housed with the wings swept fully back at 67° and staggered one behind the other. The only major restriction is that the first aircraft has to leave the shelter prior to engine start up to avoid damaging the rear aircraft.

The defence of the UKADR in peacetime is carried out in an operation known as the Quick Reaction Alert (QRA) or Q for short. RAF Leuchars is the only fighter station which has a permanent 24 hours a day, 365 days a year, Q commitment. The Q is organised in such a way that the duty squadron at the time is responsible for providing both aircraft and aircrew for Q1 and Q3, while the non duty squadron is responsible for aircraft and aircrew for Q2. Q1 and Q2 are held at 15 minutes alert whereas Q3 is on 60 minutes alert.

For QRA duty each Tornado is armed with four BAe Dynamics Skyflash medium range air-to-air missiles (AAM) and two AIM9L Sidewinder AAMs, along with the built-in 27mm Mouser cannon. This weapon is useful for firing warning shots at a potential hostile. This type of load is known as Lima fit. In addition the aircraft carry two 2250 ltr drop tanks. With the introduction of the Hardened Aircraft Shelter (HAS) the preferred method is to operate directly from the shelters, as opposed to the purpose built Q sheds of days gone by, with 111 Squadron's shelters being used regardless of which squadron holds Q duty. The reason for this is that 111's shelter complex is closer to the main Runway 09/27. Normally Q1 and Q3 are housed in the same shelter with Q3 sitting behind Q1. Aircrew for both are available on site and serve a 24 hour period of duty.

The Q Tornados are required to investigate and identify any aircraft entering the UKADR without filing a flight plan. Main trade has typically been long range Bear and Badger reconnaissance aircraft, although a few unidentified civil aircraft have also been intercepted. Only a few years past live QRA launches were an almost daily practice. The author was fortunate enough to witness a live Phantom QRA launch in September 1988. Today they are much less frequent due to the thawing of east-west relations and the break up of the former Soviet Union. In fact the Leuchars Tornados have become used to escorting Commonwealth of Independent States (CIS) aircraft visiting the station; these have included the Russian Knights aerobatic display team with their six Su27 Flanker fighters and Ilussian IL 76 Candid. The team performed their first ever full public display at Leuchars on 21 September 1991. The Russians returned in 1992 with two Su27s and a Su24MR Fencer E, the first time a Fencer had visited a front line RAF base.

On 6 September 1991 Tornado F3s from Leuchars were scrambled on the last QRA alert for a period of two years. The sleepy two year period ended on 7 September 1993, closely followed by another scramble on 17 September. The author was fortunate enough to witness this event which proved that there can still be a threat from the east. On both occasions the aircraft, a Cub and a Coot, were turned back by Norwegian AF F16A Fighting Falcons before the F3s arrived on station.

The QRA alert system would be replaced in times of crisis or war by aircraft on Combat Air Patrol (CAP). It is in this type of operation that the F3 comes into its own. A typical CAP would involve two aircraft, fully armed with four Skyflash and four Nine Limas, flying a race track pattern about 300 miles from base for a duration of 3 hours, after which they return to base or remain on station with the assistance of inflight refuelling from say a VC10 K2/3. With the combination of Marconi Foxhunter A.I. 24 radar

ZH554 GJ is caught as it retracts its undercarriage at the beginning of a sortie during Elder Joust September 1993. (Hugh Harkins)

ZE256 GA and ZE738 HA flying in formation with Su27 Flanker 389 of the CIS 19 September 1992. (Crown Copyright)

and Skyflash with its 30+ mile beyond visual range capability the Tornado F3 is one of the most capable interceptors in any air force.

Most aircraft maintenance and servicing is carried out on the base, with first line servicing of the F3s carried out at squadron level. Second line servicing (Primary star and Minor Star) is carried out by the Tornado Aircraft Servicing Flight (TASF), most of whose time is taken up with minor servicing which is due every 125 hours, and involves about 4/5 days in the TASF hangar. Usually the TASF has about three aircraft in its hangar for Minor or Primary Star servicing. During the Primary the aircraft receives a full wash down, although the rear fuselage and fin/rudder require more frequent washing because of the Tornado F3s RB199 MK104 thrust reverse buckets, which deflect the exhaust gas forwards. Major servicing, which is required every 2000 hours, is the responsibility of the Maintenance Unit (MU) at RAF St Athan. The General Engineering Flight is responsible for paint scheme touch-ups and application of squadron markings, although at any given time a number of aircraft from both squadrons can usually be observed without unit markings applied. Aircraft requiring a full repaint are normally sent to St Athan. The engineering records keep all the aircraft stabs and fatigue records on computer.

The Tornado Propulsion Flight (TPF) is a little known unit at Leuchars, whose role is to provide RB199 Mk104 engines and support for Nos 43 and 111 Squadrons and carry out all deep strip and second level work. The unit's duties include providing a replacement engine for any F3 requiring such; once a new engine is required the aircraft will be taken from the squadron's HAS complex to the TPF where a new engine will be fitted. For this a number of spare engines are stored on the base, all of which receive 100% checks by the TPF personnel. A modern purpose built building was erected for TPF in 1988; facilities include an engine bay and test house with computer controlled running procedures along with a detuner, allowing engine running even at night without annoying noise pollution. Normally an engine will be removed and a replacement installed in its place in about eight hours, although it can be, and often is, done in much less than this. In emergencies it is possible to remove an engine in under an hour and fit its replacement in a similar time scale. This capability is a far cry from the days of the Lightning and Phantom when a similar job could take days.

Most of the aircrews posted to the Tornado F3 squadrons are first tourists coming directly from the Tornado F3 Operational Conversion Unit (F3OCU) at RAF Conningsby and are declared as Limited Combat Ready (LCR). Once posted to the squadrons they have to go through a conversion exercise known as CON-VEX run by the particular squadron. This can last up to six months at the end of which the aircrew are declared combat ready. For pilots in CONVEX the first two sorties are day and night checks with the squadron QFI, later the exercise progresses to practice intercepts with 1v1, 1v2, 2v2, and 2v4, all flown at altitudes from low to high. After completion of CONVEX the aircrew are considered combat ready and therefore can take their turn on Q duty.

Away from the Tornado the only other flying unit is the Aberdeen, Dundee and St Andrews University Air Squadron (UAS) with its five BAe Bulldog T MK1s, as B flight 22 Squadron formerly equipped with two Wessex HC2s for SAR duties disbanded on 1 April 1993. The UAS formed at Leuchars in October 1981 and while all flying is done at Leuchars the H.Q. is maintained in Aberdeen. Current establishment of the unit is four qualified flying instructors and about forty students for flying training along with ten on ground training. The main aim of the UAS is flying training in about 100 hours, this takes the student up to and beyond solo spinning aerobatics, navigation instrumentation and formation flying. Airfield defence is provided by No 207 Squadron RAF Regiment, equipped with the versatile Rapier SAM system.

No 277 Squadron (Airfield Damage Repair) is a Royal Engineers Territorial Army unit whose obvious role is to repair damaged airfields.

Due to the 1990 ban on low level flying imposed by the German government, RAF Leuchars has recently had installed a fast jet turn around facility which is used by the four Tornado GR1 and two Harrier GR7 squadrons from No 2 Group RAF Strike Command (formerly RAFG). No 2 Group's aircraft fly from Leuchars to use the weapons ranges and low level training grounds on and off the coast of Scotland. The visiting aircraft flight is normally busy with the refuelling of other UK based and foreign aircraft, such as USAF F1SEs and Jaguars from RAF Coltishal. A Hercules is an almost daily sight as are tanker aircraft such as the VC10K2/3 along with the occasional Hercules C1K.

With so much activity RAF Leuchars is certainly one of the busiest operational RAF stations whose future seems to be safe from the by now hard-biting defence cuts. The two Tornado squadrons will certainly continue to provide the UKADR with its first line of defence into the twenty-first century until they are replaced by EF 2000.

QRA aircraft are loaded with a full magazine for the 27mm Mouser cannon, four Skyflash AAMs, two 2250ltr fuel tanks and two AIM9L/M sidewinders on the outboard stub pylons; this is known as Lima fit. (Hugh Harkins)

A 43 Squadron aircraft, ZE762, is moved to the 111 HAS complex for QRA duties. (Hugh Harkins)

# 7

# Tornado F3 Accidents

The Tornado F3 has proved to be a remarkably safe aircraft in RAF service, with only 4 of the 173 aircraft being lost in crashes, equivalent to approx 2.3% of the fleet. Compare this to other modern combat aircraft such as the F15, FA18 and F16 as well as the Tornado F3's predecessors, the Lightning and Phantom, and the F3 comes out well on top. Nevertheless the picture is never as rosy as it seems, the F3s have been involved in other accidents in which the aircraft have been repaired or are awaiting repair. Following are accounts of some of these accidents.

On 21 July 1989 Tornado F3 ZE833 EC of 23 Squadron RAF Leeming was lost in the type's first major crash when it hit the sea 35nm NE of Newcastle. On the morning of 21 July ZE833 led a low level interception sortie with evasion over the North Sea. There was no cloud in the operating area, but there was a haze layer from 4,500ft down to 1,000ft in which the horizon was indistinct. At 250ft the visibility was around 10km with a well defined horizon; the sea was calm but not glassy. Overall it was assessed fit for the exercise.

ZE833 led the target pair of aircraft for the first interception at 250ft and 400kts on a northerly heading. Following an uneventful intercept with the fighters positioned behind the targets, ZE833 climbed to 4,000ft, resumed a northerly heading and started to run out of the engagement. The pilot rolled the wings level and

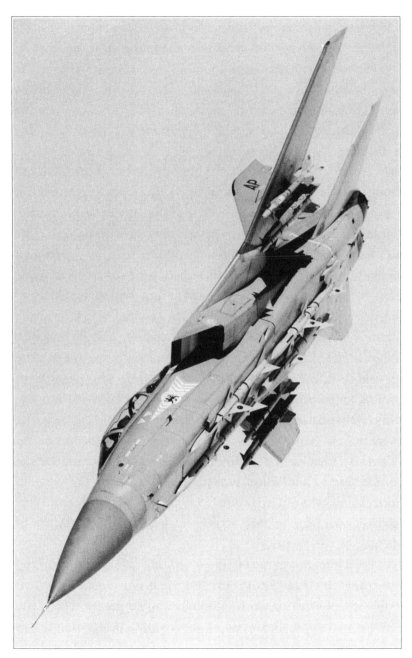

ZE 760 AP made a successful belly landing at Coningsby in June 1990 but was repaired and flying again by August. (BAe)

dropped the nose to 20–25° nose-down. As he approached 1,000ft he selected 67° sweep and began to pitch the nose up slowly. The navigator, who had been looking over his shoulder at the fighters, became aware of the lower than normal nose down attitude. He looked forward to check the altimeter, saw a reading of 3–400ft decreasing and shouted a warning to the pilot as the radar altimeter low height warning, set at 200ft, activated.

The aircraft struck the sea in a slightly nose up attitude and was immediately engulfed in a fireball. The navigator pulled his ejection seat handle just before the tail of the aircraft hit the water. He suffered minor burns as he passed through the fireball. The pilot's escape and survival equipment appear to have functioned correctly, but during the impact and ejection he sustained multiple injuries, including a very severe head injury which would have caused instant loss of consciousness. Once in the water he made no attempt to carry out any survival procedures and drowned.

The pilot failed to initiate a recovery from the descent in time to prevent the aircraft hitting the sea. It was not possible to determine the precise reason for his failure to recover, but the most likely explanation was that he had been initiating what he believed to be a smooth level-off manoeuvre from 1,000ft but did not appreciate that he was significantly undercompensating for the loss of lift due to the wings sweeping back to 67°. The smooth sea may have given him insufficient visual cues and, until the navigator's warning, he may well have been totally unaware of the danger of the situation.

A trial is being conducted on a ground proximity warning system using the radar altimeter and inertial navigation system velocities in conjunction with existing onboard computers. If the outcome is successful, RAF fast jet aircraft may be modified with this equipment.

On 7 June 1990 Tornado F3 ZE760 AP from 229 OCU Coningsby made a successful belly landing at RAF Coningsby after the pilot was unable to lower the undercarriage. The damage was only slight and was repaired in the base's aircraft servicing hangar. The aircraft was in service and flying again by August.

On 11 March 1991 Coningsby based ZE728 AN from 229 OCU departed RAF Coningsby as part of a three ship formation, transiting to the training area over the North Sea. The aircraft was using the call sign Lucky 1 and events were to show that the crew were lucky on more than one occasion. ZE728 had a lucky escape when the pilot accidentally fired his ejection seat drogue while on a training sortie over the North Sea, holing the canopy and deploying his 5ft diameter drogue parachute which almost dragged him out of the cockpit. ZE728 is a dual control aircraft, therefore when the navigator could not make contact with or confirm the pilot's condition, he decided to take control of the aircraft. The pilot was later able to communicate with the navigator by means of hand signals, helping him to keep control of the aircraft.

The Tornado's home base, Coningsby, was contacted and alerted by the navigator, although due to the severe noise of the rushing air the station's controllers were not made fully aware of the seriousness of the situation. As the aircraft headed for home the problems started: first the crew encountered breathing problems, therefore it was decided to use the emergency oxygen supply. As he was reaching for the oxygen handle the pilot noticed his right leg restraint garter was tangled near the knee, while trying to free it he accidentally activated the seat Manual Separation Lever (MSL). This resulted in the drogue gun piston firing through the canopy, following which the pilot's drogue chute deployed into the aircraft's slipstream and plumed over the rear canopy and spine; luckily it partially collapsed as it snagged on the aircraft's tailfin.

Fortunately the pilot had been unable to free his tangled gaiter as this is all that saved him from being totally dragged from the cockpit through the hole that had been punched in the canopy, although if the drogue had not tangled itself on the fin it would certainly have pulled the pilot from the cockpit.

As the controllers vectored ZE728 to runway 26 the Tornado was struggling to maintain altitude, crossing the Lincolnshire coast at 300ft with about 20 miles still to go to Coningsby. Once again problems were encountered as the drogue bloomed again on approach to the airfield, pulling the main parachute from the pack attached to the pilot's back. Once more luck was with the pilot as the chute billowed around his head and back rather than up through the hole in the canopy. As the pilot was still unable to fly the aircraft it was left to the navigator to land ZE728.

Operating his harness quick-release in an attempt to get clear of the seat parachute harness, the pilot found that the harness still remained trapped and to make matters worse still, his personal survival pack, which he would normally be sitting on, had become partially upturned.

Despite all the problems and the pilot's awkward position the navigator still managed to land the aircraft safely, although as it touched down the pilot's harness was ripped from the cockpit out through the open canopy by the billowing parachute, causing temporary loss of directional control. Despite this the navigator was still able to keep the aircraft straight on the runway until the pilot selected dump and full reverse thrust bringing the aircraft to a halt.

Once the aircraft had came to a halt the emergency service repinned the still armed front seat through the smashed canopy glass in order to make it safe. Some time later the crew were able to leave the aircraft feeling fit enough to walk back to the crew room. After being made safe, the aircraft was moved to a remote part of the base to undergo further checks, during which it was found that the pilot's ejection seat firing handle had been partially pulled from its housing.

An inquiry into the incident has been conducted as this was similar to the incident which resulted in the loss of Harrier GR5 ZD325 on 22 October 1987, when while still being operated by BAe, the pilot was killed when dragged out of the aircraft after the Manual Separation Lever had activated. The Harrier flew on for some 90 miles before crashing into the Atlantic.

On 16 July 1992 a pair of Leeming Wing Tornado F3s, ZE158 EC from 23 Squadron and ZE159 DC from 11 Squadron, were involved in a mid air collision over the North Sea, 20 miles north-east of Newcastle. Luckily both pilots were able to retain control of their aircraft and make emergency landings at Newcastle Airport.

The two Tornado F3s touched each other whilst conducting simultaneous overland practice interception sorties over Northumberland. Both aircraft suffered only minor damage and there were no injuries. The occurrence was therefore categorised as an air incident. The Ministry of Defence does not normally summarise the investigations of air incidents for publication. However the potential seriousness of this particular air incident merited the level of investigation normally reserved for air accidents.

The two aircraft were members of two separate formations, each of three aircraft. Each formation was aware of the other's presence and had been briefed on measures to deconflict their activities. The sorties progressed normally until one formation initiated a practice interception on the other, using its onboard

ZH558 GF of 43 Squadron during Elder Joust 16 September 1993. This aircraft was lost off Cyprus on July 8th 1994. (Hugh Harkins)

ZE252 HH was one of the batch of aircraft damaged by Airwork during maintenance in early 1993. (Hugh Harkins)

radar equipment. The formations were heading towards each other, separated in height from the southern and northerly ends of the operating area, with the southerly formation intercepting the northerly one.

The northerly formation leader recognised the possibility of confliction and advised his opposite number by means of radio which was made on his behalf by another member of his formation. The southerly formation leader accordingly ordered the break of the interception. The leading pair of his formation immediately commenced a climbing turn away, but the No 3 in the southerly formation, three and half miles in trail, continued on a northerly heading in order to maintain formation integrity and inexplicably continued to descend.

As the range closed, both crews (the leader in the northerly formation and the No 3 in the southerly formation) switched their attention from radar to visual lookout. Both saw the other two aircraft in the opposing formations displaced on their right hand sides, but failed to see each other. The pilot of the northernmost aircraft did however see the other aircraft shortly before the impact and manoeuvred his aircraft hard in an attempt to avoid it.

The aircraft touched at a height of 2000ft (610m). The tail of one aircraft struck the underside of the other aircraft causing minor damage to both. ZE159 suffered underfuselage damage resulting in an engine fire as the aircraft landed, while ZE158 lost a large chunk of its tailfin. The damage sustained did not cause any handling difficulties and both pilots landed their aircraft at Newcastle airport.

The incident was caused by the failure of both crews to see each other in sufficient time to take avoiding action. When practice interception was called off the No 3 in the southerly formation continued his descent to co-altitude with the other aircraft.

Furthermore, he did not break off the interception when instructed by his leader.

Standard operating procedures have since been adopted for Tornado crews conducting tactical training overland, which include specific instruction for the airborne co-ordinating of formations. Disciplinary action has been taken against both crews involved in the incident.

ZE159 EC was soon flying again and flew back to RAF Leeming on 28 July. It had received a new fin tip but still required speed tape to cover temporarily other minor damage. Also the RHWR had a slight downward tilt indicating that this too had been damaged. ZE159 has received the EG code, partly it is said, due to two former EC aircraft having suffered accidents. The other example was involved in a heavy landing in 1988. ZE158DC is still in the AMF at Leeming, having arrived from Newcastle by road on 3 August, but will be repaired and should be flying again by the middle of 1994.

In a totally unconnected incident another F3 ZE888 EV from 23 Squadron was forced to divert to Newcastle following a bird strike on the same day.

Also in July a III Squadron Tornado, F3 ZE289 HF, suffered a nosewheel collapse after landing at Leuchars. The collapse caused substantial buckling of the front fuselage. In the first half of 1993 the aircraft remained in the Leuchars ASF hangar to await a decision on its fate. It is probable that the aircraft will be declared Cat 5.

Staying with Leuchars, during the early summer another III Squadron Tornado F3 was involved in an accident. ZE250 HZ suffered serious damage due to an engine fire although the full extent of the damage is still unconfirmed, as is the aircraft's fate.

An official report published by the Joint Airmiss Working Group (JAWG) on a near miss involving a Tornado F3 of 56R Squadron RAF and a Civilian Piper PA–34 Seneca has strongly criticised the Air Traffic Controllers (ATC). The report stated that none of the controllers involved in the incident were to undertake screening duties until their competence had been checked although all had been returned to duty. On 19 August 1992 four 56R Squadron Tornado F3s were temporarily based at RAF Waddington, for DACT with Harrier GR7s of No 4 Squadron and 233 OCU 20R Squadron. The Tornados made a stream take-off and were initially warned by a controller to stay below 3000ft (900m) until the Seneca had cleared the airfield. However a colleague then lifted the height restriction without telling the original controller and as a result the Tornados started to climb higher with one of them closing on the Seneca from below on what appeared to be a potential collision course. The pilot of one of the other Tornados was the first to see the Seneca which was flying at 4500ft and immediately warned the first Tornado pilot, who had seen the potential collision a mere split second before and quickly rolled the Tornado away.

The ensuing enquiry found that there was a high ATC workload just before the potential collision, with 45 messages in 90 seconds between ATC and aircraft. In addition the supervising controller was distracted while arranging a relief break for staff. It was also noted that radar imagery might not have been clear on the controller's screen, a back-up system had been used as Waddington's primary radar had failed. The enquiry found the ATC guilty of failing to pass sufficient information to the civilian pilot and of poor judgment.

It was estimated that the two aircraft involved in the near miss came within a few feet of each other and the incident was put into the rare A Cat of air miss. This classification actually means that there existed a real possibility of a collision had no evasive action been taken. It is claimed that the Tornado passed so close that the pilot and passengers of the Seneca were thrown from their seats by the fighter's jetwash and the Seneca pilot actually thought that the aircraft had hit each other, therefore he diverted into Waddington where his aircraft was inspected and found to be undamaged.

Although it was not an accident, more a case of unintentional sabotage, the RAF had effectively to ground eighteen of its Tornado F3 fleet after the discovery of some serious damage to the airedales following servicing by a private contractor. As in all work in these days of competitive tendering, the MOD has contracted out airframe modification work to increase the FI of its Tornado F3 fleet, the first contract for 15 aircraft which was won by BAe having already been carried out satisfactorily.

The second such contract for a total of 18 aircraft was won by Airwork Services for a price of £7m. which was £4m. less than BAe. With the discovery of the damage the MOD immediately cancelled the contract. The work was being done at RAF St Athan and a report by the local MP on 4 June stated that due to delays in completing the contract Airwork personnel began using inappropriate tools for the work.

It is reported that longerons were distorted when pneumatic guns, similar to those used to remove nuts from car wheels, were used to remove light alloy collars covering the nuts and bolts holding panels to the longerons, thus causing the collars to be almost chiselled off.

The damage was discovered by RAF maintenance personnel after pilots reported problems with the first four aircraft returned to the squadrons. This resulted in tests being done on the remaining fourteen aircraft at RAF St Athan where twelve were found to be seriously damaged while the other two were slightly damaged.

ZE858 GO a few weeks before it crashed on 21.10.93. (Hugh Harkins)

In late May the aircraft were inspected by officials from DASA, the German Panavia partner, who were said to be horrified at what they saw. It was suggested that the 12 most damaged aircraft may have to return to Germany in order for their centre fuselages to be rebuilt in the original manufacturing jigs so as to restore structural strength.

The four aircraft that were delivered to their units, ZE292, ZE295, ZE343 and ZE728 have since been returned to St Athan for repair, although by early 1994 it was announced that 14 of the 18 aircraft affected were to be prematurely scrapped. Another possibility was to use the centre fuselages from the Tornado F2s stored at RAF St. Athan. The 25 FI structural updating programme was immediately halted after the discovery of the damage but RAF personnel had the conversion line going again four weeks later and in the first half of 1994 three aircraft, Z163, 200 and 789 had been returned to service with 56R, 11 and 56R Squadrons respectively. On 16 September 1994 the RAF was awarded the follow-on contract for the updating program.

On 21 October 1993 ZE858 GO of 43 Squadron was on a routine training sortie from RAF Leuchars when it crashed, both crew ejected safely before the aircraft crashed in open ground on the border between Cumbria and Co. Durham.

The aircraft was part of a defensive formation of four Tornado F3s escorting two Tornado GR1 fighter bombers on a training sortie on which they were pitted against four attacking Tornado F3s from another station. They were to operate in the UK low flying system in the Pennines region. Some 40 minutes into the sortie the aircraft suffered a massive fuel leak which caused a severe loss of power to the left engine. As the pilot initiated recovery to a diversion airfield he selected full reheat on both engines to climb away from low level. Unfortunately this ignited the vapour trail of fuel that was leaking from the aircraft and caused fires, first in the right engine jet pipe and within minutes in the left engine jet pipe. Unable to extinguish the fires and with both engines shut down, the crew ejected successfully, having first pointed the aircraft in a direction to avoid the A66 main road. The aircraft crashed in moorland adjacent to the road.

The accident investigation determined that the fuel leak had occurred in the engine fuel system. A clamp used in the connection of the feed pipe to an engine component had fractured. However it was concluded that the primary cause of the accident was the selection of reheat, which caused the ignition of the leaking fuel and subsequent jet pipe fires. The failure of the fuel feed pipe clamp and the inability to extinguish the jet pipe fires were both considered to have contributed to the accident.

The RAF engineering support authority for the Tornado has issued regular inspection requirements, pending the result of an investigation by the makers into the nature of the failure of the V clamp. A review of in-service maintenance procedures for all similar types of clamps is underway.

This was followed on 7 June 1994 by ZE809 HP of 111 Squadron which crashed while operating with 11 Squadron of the Leeming wing. The aircraft caught fire during a sortie from Leeming, both crew members ejected and the aircraft crashed into the North Sea 60 miles (97km) north-east of Newcastle, the crew were picked up by a 202 Squadron Sea King HAR3.

The last of the three accidents involved one of the youngest F3s, ZH558 was the penultimate Tornado F3 and had been in service for little over a year. The aircraft, coded GF, crashed into the Mediterranean Sea 15 miles (24km) South of Cyprus where it was based during an extended 7 week Armament Practice Camp due to runway repairs at its home base of RAF Leuchars.

# Appendices
## Table 1

### Variants

Tornado F2    Three prototypes and 18 interim production aircraft with MK103 engine.

Tornado F3    152 standard production aircraft with uprated MK104 engine.

The RAF had an initial requirement for 165 Tornado ADV of which the first 3 aircraft were to be prototypes and be added to Batch 1. Of the Batch 6 aircraft, 24 were diverted to fulfil an order from the RSAF, being replaced from Batch 7 production. The RAF ordered a further 15 aircraft to be delivered from Batch 8 but 7 of these were subsequently cancelled under the 1990 options for changes in defence cuts. The remaining 8 were delivered from Batch 8 with the RAF taking delivery of its last Tornado ADV F MK3 in March 1993. As there were differences, particularly in the standard of radar software between aircraft of the same production Batch, this resulted in Block numbers becoming important. The 18 aircraft from Batch 4 production were the only ADV completed as interim F MK2s.

| | Standard | Dual Control | Total | First Flight |
|---|---|---|---|---|
| Batch 1 Block 1 | 2 | 1 | 3 | 27.10.79 |
| Batch 4 Block 8 | 0 | 6 | 6 | 12.4.84 |
| Batch 4 Block 9 | 10 | 2 | 12 | 11.1.85 |
| Batch 5 Block 10 | 12 | 6 | 18 | 20.11.85 |
| Batch 5 Block 11 | 22 | 12 | 34 | 26.8.86 |
| Batch 6 Block 12 | 39 | 7 | 46 | 9.87 |
| Batch 6 Block 13 | 12 | 10 | 22 | 1.12.88 |
| Batch 7 Block 14 | 7 | 0 | 7 | 1990 |
| Batch 7 Block 15 | 17 | 0 | 17 | 1991 |
| Batch 8 Block 16 | 0 | 8 | 8 | 2.92 |
| TOTALS | 121 | 52 | 173 | |

A pair of 5 Squadron Tornado F3s, ZE254CA foreground and ZG730CC. (BAe)

# Table 2

## Specification

Type            All weather long range interceptor.

Powerplant      Two Turbo Union RB199 MK104 turbofan en-
                gines each rated at 9,656lb (42.9kn) dry and
                16,920lb (75.2kn) with reheat.

Dimensions      Wings—Span unswept 45ft 7.5in (13.91m)
                Span swept 28ft 2.5in (8.60m).
                Wing area unswept 322.93sq ft (30.00m2).
                Wing sweep 25 to 67°.
                Length 59ft 3.8in (18.08m); height 19ft.
                6.25in (5.95m);

Weights         Empty 31,970lb (14501kg); max take-off 61,700lb.
                (27987kg).

Loadings        At normal take-off weight: wing 155lb sq ft
                (759kg/m2); thrust 0.67; G limits 7.5g.

Landing Gear    Retractable tricycle configuration with single main
                gear units and twin steerable nose wheels.
                Wheel base 20ft 4in (6.20); wheel track 10ft 2in.
                (3.10m).

Fuel            Internal 12,500lb (5670kg); fuel fraction 0.25.

Performance    Max speed Mach 2.2+ 1,452mph (2337km/h) at altitude; Mach 1.2 921mph at sea level; initial climb rate 40,000ft per min (203m per sec); service ceiling 50,000ft (15250m); interception radius subsonic 1,151 miles (1853km); supersonic 354 miles (556km) +; take off run 2,500ft (762m); landing run 1,215ft (370m).

Armament    Four Skyflash BVR missiles and four AIM9L Sidewinder heat seeking missiles for shorter range engagements, a single 27mm cannon is used for really close work; in the future the AIM 120 AMRAAM active BVR missile will be deployed.

Crew    One pilot and one navigator

# Table 3

## Battle Of Britain 50th Anniversary Fly-past

| | | |
|---|---|---|
| ZE160 HA 111 Sqn | ZE166 CT 5 Sqn | ZE207 BJ 29 Sqn |
| ZE209 AS 65 Sqn | ZE253 AB 65 Sqn | ZE256 AJ 65 Sqn |
| ZE257 BD 29 Sqn | ZE290 25 Sqn | ZE291 AZ 65 Sqn |
| ZE338 BB 29 Sqn | ZE340 AG 65 Sqn | ZE342 BK 29 Sqn |
| ZE728 BS 29 Sqn | ZE730 DF 11 Sqn | ZE733 FH 25 Sqn |
| ZE735 FE 25 Sqn | ZE760 CF 5 Sqn | ZE761 CC 5 Sqn |
| ZE785 DA 11 Sqn | ZE789 DD 11 Sqn | ZE791 FF 25 Sqn |
| ZE793 DZ 11 Sqn | ZE808 DJ 11 Sqn | ZE809 EZ 23 Sqn |
| ZE811 DI 11 Sqn | ZE812 EA 23 Sqn | ZE830 ET 23 Sqn |
| ZE831 EW 23 Sqn | ZE836 EF 23 Sqn | ZE837 EA 25 Sqn |
| ZE838 FA 25 Sqn | ZE858 FB 25 Sqn | |

Before buying the Tornado F3 the RAF first looked at other off the shelf designs including the F15 Eagle. While the Eagle was a highly manoeuvrable aircraft optimised for agility the RAF felt that APG-63 radar was incapable of operating in the dense high clutter environment for which the Foxhunter on Tornado was designed. Also the Eagle was shorter ranged and the one man crew was deemed a disadvantage. (Hugh Harkins)

Entering service with the Soviet (now Russian) and CIS forces in increasing numbers during the late 1980s, the Su27 Flanker is a highly agile aircraft but its advantage over Tornado F3 ends there. (Hugh Harkins)

# Table 4

## Combat Comparisons

### Max Speed at Altitude

| | | |
|---|---|---|
| Tornado F3 | – | Mach 2.2 |
| F15 Eagle | – | Mach 2.5 |
| Mirage 2000C | – | Mach 2.2 |
| Su 27 Flanker | – | Mach 2.35 |
| Mig 31 Foxhound | – | Mach 2.4 |
| FA18 Hornet | – | Mach 1.8 |
| F16 | – | Mach 2 |
| F14A Tomcat | – | Mach 2.31 |

### Max Speed Sea Level

| | | |
|---|---|---|
| Tornado F3 | – | Mach 1.2 |
| F15 Eagle | – | Mach 1.2 |
| Mirage 2000C | – | Mach 1.2 |
| Su27 Flanker | – | Mach 1.2 |
| Mig 31 Foxhound | – | Mach 1.1 |
| FA18 Hornet | – | Mach 1 |
| F16 Falcon | – | Mach 1 |
| F14 Tomcat | – | Mach 1.2 |

### Service Ceiling

| | | |
|---|---|---|
| Tornado F3 | – | 50,000ft |
| F15C Eagle | – | 65,000ft |

| | | |
|---|---|---|
| Mirage 2000C | – | 60,000ft |
| Su 27 Flanker | – | 59,058ft |
| Mig 31 Foxhound | – | 75,000ft |
| FA18 Hornet | – | 50,000ft |
| F16C Falcon | – | 50,000ft |
| F14A Tomcat | – | 56,000ft |

## Initial Climb Rate

| | | |
|---|---|---|
| Tornado F3 | – | 40,000ft/min |
| F15C Eagle | – | 50,000ft/min |
| Mirage 2000C | – | 49,212ft/min |
| Su 27 Flanker | – | 60,000ft/min |
| Mig 31 Foxhound | – | 41,000ft/min |
| FA18C Hornet | – | 50,000ft/min |
| F16C Falcon | – | 50,000ft/min |
| F14A Tomcat | – | 30,000ft/min |

## Combat Radius

| | | |
|---|---|---|
| Tornado F3 | – | 1,151nm |
| F15C Eagle | – | 500nm |
| Mirage 2000C | – | 300nm |
| Su 27 Flanker | – | 810nm |
| Mig 31 Foxhound | – | 1135nm |
| FA18C Hornet | – | 575nm |
| F16C Falcon | – | 500nm |
| F14A Tomcat | – | 750nm |

## G Limits

| | | |
|---|---|---|
| Tornado F3 | – | +7.5 |
| F15C Eagle | – | +9 |
| Mirage 2000 | – | +9 |

Su 27 Flanker — +9
Mig 31 Foxhound — About 6
FA18C Hornet — +9
F16C Falcon — +9
F14A Tomcat — +7.5

## Radar Comparisons

Tornado F MK3   AI24 Foxhunter Operates I band, can track up to 20 targets while still searching for others, range 120 miles.

F15C   APG—63 range 160nm (296km) operates I/J band.

Mirage 2000C   Early aircraft Thompson CSF RDM I band track while scan capable of locating 90% of fighter sized targets within 45nm (85km 53 miles) assuming a 5m2 (54sq ft) surface.

Su 27 Flanker B   RLPK—27 detection range 149 miles (240km), tracking range 115 miles (185km), can track ten targets simultaneously; once locked on to a target the radar cannot continue to scan for or track others.

Mig 31 Foxhound   SBI—16 Zaslon with reporting name Flash Dance, probably operates in I or G bands; can track ten targets selecting the four threatening targets, detection range of 16m2 (172sq ft) target is 124 miles (200km) with a tracking range of 74 miles (120km).

FA18C Hornet   APG—65 Can track ten targets displaying eight range 80nm.

F16C Falcon      APG–68 inferior to APG–65, most F16s have no BVR capability.

F14A Tomcat      AWG–9 Can track 24 targets while engaging 6 and continuing to search for others, range 150 miles (340km).

## Combat Persistence

Tornado F MK3      Internal 27mm cannon four Skyflash BVR and four AIM9L/M Sidewinder AAMs. The F3 does not use its outboard underwing pylons but this could change with the introduction of the AIM120 AMRAAM which is to replace Skyflash with one being carried on each pylon for a total of six. If the decision not to issue the new AIM132 ASRAAM short range AAM to F3 Squadrons is reversed then the outboard pylons could each carry three of these small AAMs along with the four on the inboard pylons and the four AMRAAMS, this would give a total of 14 AAMs true combat persistence.

F15C Eagle      Internal 20mm six barrel cannon, four each of AIM7M Sparrow or AIM120 AMRAAM and AIM9L/M Sidewinder AAMs, or up to eight AMRAAMs. Some aircraft have flown operationally with a mix of AMRAAMs, Sparrows and Sidewinders.

Mirage 2000C      Internal 30mm cannon and two Matra super 530D SARH and two Matra R550 Magic MK2 AAMs.

Su 27 Flanker B — Internal 30mm cannon four R73 AA11 Archer short range infra red AAMs and six R27 AA10 Alamo BVR AAMs. The R27 is available in IR and SARH versions.

Mig 31 Foxhound — Internal 23mm six barrel cannon, four R33 AA9 Amos SARH BVR AAM and either a pair of R40 AA6 Acrids, one each in SARH and IR, or four AA8 Aphids. The Mig 31 does not normally have its outboard underwing pylons fitted but could carry another four AA8s or a pair of AA6s if fitted.

FA18C Hornet — Internal 20mm six barrel cannon and two AIM7M Sparrow AAM and six AIM9L/M Sidewinder AAM. With the introduction of the AIM120 AMRAAM the FA18 has been successfully flown with a total of ten AMRAAMs and two AIM9s.

F16C Falcon — Internal 20mm six barrel cannon and four AIM9L/M and two AIM7M or AMRAAM AAMs. Alternatively a load of six AMRAAMs can be carried.

F14A Tomcat — Internal 20mm six barrel cannon, six long range AIM54 Phoenix AAMs or 4 AIM54s and 2 each of AIM7M Sparrow Medium range AAMs and AIM9L/M Sidewinder short range AAMs; or 4 AIM7s and 4 AIM9s. With the introduction of the AIM120 AMRAAM up to eight of these fire and forget missiles can be carried.

# Table 5

## Aircraft Involved In Desert Shield/Storm

ZE158 (D) +; 159 (DO-O) +-; 160 (Z) +; 161 (DR-R) +; 162 (DM) +; 163+; 164 (DQ-G) +; 165 (DU-U) +; 200 (DZ-W) +; 203 (DA) +; 204 (B) +; 205 (BF); 206 (D-C) +; 208 (DC) + 210 (DD) +; 254 (BG); 255 (BH); 258 (BE); 289 (BA); 338 (BB); 732 (CH); 734 (CJ); 736 (CK); 758 (CB); 762 (CA); 763 (BA) +; 764 (I) +; 887 (C) +; 888 (DT-K) +-; 907+; 908 (X) +; 934 (DV-Q) +; 936 (DF-F) +; 941 (DW) +; 961 (DH-H) +; 962 (DI) +; 963 (DX) +; 964 (DS) +; 965 (DY) +; 96 (GF) +; 967 (DR) +; 968 (DJ-J) +; 969 (DL-L) +; 982 (DP-P) +-

# Table 6

## Aircraft Involved In Operation Deny Flight

ZE164 (DA) +; ZE206 (EW) +; ZE210 (FB) +; ZE808 (FA) +; ZE936 (EE) +; ZE961 (FD) +. As well as the aircraft mentioned above most of the pool of aircraft upgraded to Stage 1+ are being rotated through Gio del Colle.

# Table 7

## Units Operating the Tornado F2/3

| | |
|---|---|
| 29 OCU/65R Sqn Coningsby | – 1.5.85–1.7.92 |
| Tornado F3 OEU Coningsby | – 1.4.87–Present |
| 29 Sqn Coningsby | – 4.87–Present |
| 5 Sqn Coningsby | – 1.1.88–Present |
| 11 Sqn Leeming | – 1.5.88–Present |
| 23 Sqn Leeming | – 1.11.88–26.2.94 |
| 25 Sqn Leeming | – 1.7.89–Present |
| 43 Sqn Leuchars | – 9.89–Present |
| 111 Sqn Leuchars | – 1.5.90–Present |
| 1435FLT Mount Pleasant FI | – 6.92–Present |
| F3 OCU/56R Sqn | – 1.7.92–Present |

Other test agencies or companies have operated one or more Tornado F2/3s these being: MOD(PE) BAe Warton, MOD(PE) A&AEE Bascombe Down, MOD(PE) DRA Farnborough now Bascombe Down, and the Empire Test Pilots School Bascombe Down.

The Tornado F3 is a remarkably small aircraft compared to other aircraft in its class such as the F14 Tomcat and Mig 31 Foxhound. (Hugh Harkins)

# Individual Aircraft Histories

ZA254     F/f 9.8.79, BAe; A&AEE, BAe Warton.

ZA267T     F/F 18.7.80, BAe, A&AEE Bascombe Down.

ZA283     F/f 18.11.80, BAe Warton.

ZD899T     F/f 12.4.84; A&AEE A Squadron; BAe Warton. Flew in formation with EF2000 prototype DA2 ZH588 at BAe Warton 4.5.94.

ZD900T     F/f 5.3.84; A&AEE A Squadron.

ZD901T     F/f 14.6.84; AA 229 OCU Coningsby 5.11.84, Was first F2 for No 229 OCU together with ZD903; AB 229 OCU Coningsby 7.87; St Athan for storage 19.10.87; to be scrapped under 1993 cuts.

ZD902T     F/f 4.9.84; AC229 OCU Coningsby 5.85; with DRA Farnborough as a trials aircraft for A.D equipment. Was redesignated an F2A by 9.94 and at same time relocated to Bascombe Down.

ZD903T     F/f 21.9.84; AB 229 OCU 5.11.84; Together with ZD901 was first F2 for 229 OCU; St Athan for storage 16.11.87; to be scrapped under 1993 cuts.

ZD904T     F/f 30.1.85; AE 229 OCU Coningsby 5.85; to St Athan for storage 1.88; to be scrapped under 1993 cuts.

ZD905     F/f 11.1.85; A&AEE A Squadron 4.85; AV 229 OCU 21.10.85; St Athan for storage 1987.

ZD906     F/f 5.2.85; AN 229 OCU 5.85; St Athan for storage 3.86.

ZD932     F/f 22.3.85; AM 229 OCU Coningsby 5.85; St Athan for storage 11.3.87; to be scrapped under 1993 cuts.

ZD933     F/f 16.4.85; AO 229 OCU Coningsby 5.85; loaned to St Athan for familiarisation 10.1.86—13.3.86; St Athan for storage 3.86; to be scrapped under 1993 cuts.

ZD934T     F/f 17.4.85; AD 229 OCU 6.85; St Athan for storage 25.9.87; to be scrapped under 1993 cuts.

ZD935T     F/f 16.5.85; AF 229 OCU 7.85; stored 1.88.

ZD936     F/f 14.6.85; 229 OCU Coningsby 7.8.85; spares source; AP 229 OCU Coningsby 2.86; St Athan for storage 4.3.87; to be scrapped under 1993 cuts.

ZD937     F/f 28.6.85; AQ 229 OCU 8.85; St Athan for storage 8.12.86; St Athan BDRT coded A.

ZD938     F/f 2.8.85; AR 229 OCU Coningsby 2.9.85; St Athan 24.4.87; to be scrapped under 1993 cuts.

ZD939     F/f 8.8.85; AS 229 OCU Coningsby 9.85; St Athan 2.87; BAe Warton; BAe Warton instructional use by 4.94.

ZD940     F/f 19.8.85; AT 229 OCU Coningsby 2.10.85; St Athan 9.1.87; to be scrapped under 1993 cuts.

ZD941     F/f 2.9.85; AU 229 OCU Coningsby 9.10.85; stored RAF St Athan by 9.1.87.

ZE154T     F/f 20.11.85; BAe Warton; A&AEE 24.12.85; BAe Warton; ASF Coningsby 7.87; AK 229 OCU Coningsby 9.87; AD 229 OCU Coningsby 1992; AD 56R Squadron Coningsby by 10.92; stored at St Athan by 7.93.

ZE155     F/f 16.10.86; BAe Warton (JTIDS trials); was the first F3 to cross Atlantic assisted by Tristar K MK1 9.87; to Yuma Arizona for trials 9.87; was first British fighter to cross Atlantic without inflight refuelling; flew Goose Bay Canada to Warton, a distance of 2,200 miles, in a time of 4hrs 45 min 24.9.87; A&AEE

Bascombe Down went to Khamis Mushayt air base, Saudi Arabia, in 1991 to conduct hot weather altitude and weight trials with various loads including an additional two 1500 ltr tanks under the fuselage. 1992 still with A&AEE. MOD(PE) BAe Warton by 9.94.

ZE156    Delayed on line for installation of test equipment; AM 229 OCU Coningsby 3.3.87; first OCU aircraft with revised nose arrowhead markings 4.87; re-coded AV still with OCU 11.87; FJ 25 Squadron Leeming; FJ St Athan by 8.91 used for Mid Life Overhaul (MLO) trials; HE 111 Squadron Leuchars, 1992.

ZE157T    F/f 14.1.86; A&AEE 20.4.86; AH 229 OCU 10.86; AB 229 OCU Coningsby; AB 56R Squadron Coningsby by 10.92; stored St Athan by 7.93. A156R Squadron Coningsby by 5.94.

ZE158    F/f 25.9.86; 229 OCU 30.10.86; AK 229 OCU Coningsby; this aircraft was the first to be decorated with the 229 OCU red yellow arrow on its fin top 12.86; re-coded AP still with OCU 8.87; Leeming wing; D 11 Squadron Dhahran by 11.90; modified to S1+; 43 Squadron Leuchars by 1.91; BFME by 2.91; DC 11 Squadron Leeming by 5.91; on 16.7.92 the aircraft was involved in a mid air collision with ZE159, having suffered damage it diverted to Newcastle and was returned to Leeming by road on 3.8.92. The aircraft is in the AMF at Leeming awaiting repair.

ZE159    F/f 27.6.86; AW 229 OCU 28.7.86; first F3 for 229 OCU 28.7.86; St Athan 12.1.88; Leeming wing; DO 11 Squadron Dhahran 21–22.9.90; modified to S1+; O BFME EC 23 Squadron Leeming by 7.91, was involved in mid air collision with ZE158, diverted to

Newcastle airport and flew back to Leeming on 28.7.92 and was later coded EG.

ZE160T    F/f 2.7.86; AG 229 OCU 8.8.86; HA 111 Squadron Leuchars; took part in BBF as HA 111 Squadron; Z 11 Squadron Leeming by 1.91; 29 Squadron Coningsby by 7.91; EX 23 Squadron Leeming by 5.93; 25 Squadron Leeming by 4.94; DV 11 Squadron Leeming by 7.94.

ZE161     F/f 7.7.86; AX 229 OCU Coningsby 1.8.86; GI 43 Squadron Leuchars by 8.90; DN 11 Squadron Dhahran by October 90; modified to S1+; R BFME FG 25 Squadron Leeming by 7.91; 25 Squadron Leeming by 5.93.

ZE162     F/f 16.7.86; AY 229 OCU 13.8.86; AY 229 OCU Coningsby; St Athan 20.11.87; AW 229 OCU Coningsby; DM 11 Squadron Dhahran on 16–17.9.90; modified to S1+; M 11 Squadron Leeming by 1.91; FK 25 Squadron Leeming 1992.

ZE163T    F/f 6.7.87; AL 229 OCU 11.9.87; AL 229 OCU Coningsby; CF 5 Squadron Coningsby by 8.90; CF 5C Squadron Dhahran 8.90; 111 Squadron Leuchars by 5.91; A2 229 OCU Coningsby by 10.91; AA 56R Squadron Coningsby by 10.92.

ZE164     F/f 22.7.86; AN 229 OCU Coningsby 18.9.86; AU 229 OCU Coningsby 1.88; AN 229 OCU Coningsby; HH 111 Squadron Leuchars; DQ 11 Squadron Dhahran by 11.90; modified to S1+; G BFME; G 11 Squadron Leeming by 5.91; DA 11 Squadron Leeming by 7.91.

ZE165     F/f 11.8.86; AZ 229 OCU Coningsby 8.9.86; AZ 229 OCU Coningsby; HL 111 Squadron Leuchars; DU 11

Squadron Dhahran by 21–22.9.90; modified to S1+; U BFME: BJ 29 Squadron Coningsby; FO 25 Squadron Leeming by 7.93.

ZE166T    F/f 27.10.86; AI 229 OCU Coningsby 12.11.86; CT 5 Squadron Coningsby; BBF as CT 5 Squadron; AF 229 OCU; AF 56R Squadron Coningsby by 10.92.

ZE167    F/f 2.10.86; delivered 23.10.86; re-coded AR 9.87; AL 229 OCU; 25 Squadron Leeming by 5.91; HM 111 Squadron Leuchars by 12.91; HM A&AEE Bascombe Down. HX 111 Squadron Leuchars by 10.94.

ZE168    F/f 31.10.86; AO 229 OCU 18.11.86; AO 229 OCU Coningsby; 23 Squadron Leeming by 5.91; EB 23 Squadron Leeming; EB 25 Squadron Leeming by 7.94.

ZE199    F/f 19.11.86; AJ 229 OCU19.12.86; DQ 11 Squadron Leeming by 8.90; DQ 111 Squadron Leuchars by 1.91; W 11 Squadron Leeming by 1.91; 43 Squadron Leuchars 14.3.91; FL 25 Squadron Leeming by 7.91.

ZE200    F/f 24.2.87; ASF 6.3.87; A&AEE Bascombe Down 5.87; AS 229 OCU 1.9.87; AV 229 OCU Coningsby; DZ 11 Squadron Dhahran by 10.90; modified to S1+ for Gulf ops but remained at Leeming; L BFME DB 11 Squadron Leeming; DB stored St Athan by 7.93; 11 Squadron Coningsby by 6.94.

ZE201    F/f 4.12.86; AQ 229 OCU Coningsby 17.12.86; AQ 229 OCU Coningsby 1990; E 11 Squadron Leeming by 1.91; E 43 Squadron Leuchars on 14.3.91; ED 23 Squadron Leeming by 7.91; stored St Athan by 7.93.

ZE202T    F/f 26/27.8.86; A&AEE 12.9.86; AH 229 OCU Coningsby; AH 56R Squadron Coningsby by 10.92; AG 56R Squadron Coningsby by 3.93.

ZE203     F/f 28/29.8.86; delivered 30.9.86; AO 229 OCU 12.9.86; ASF Coningsby 4.87; BA 29 Squadron Coningsby 6.87; AO 229 OCU Coningsby; FI 25 Squadron Leeming; DA 11 Squadron Dhahran on 21–22.9.90; modified to S1+; A 25 Squadron Leeming by 5.91; FI 25 Squadron Leeming by 7.91; borrowed by Leuchars wing April 92 and took part in first F3 deployment to Alaska for Distant Frontier 92 flown by 111 and 43 Squadrons.

ZE204     F/f 10.9.86; ASF Coningsby 15.10.86; BB 29 Squadron 6.87; GJ 43 Squadron Leuchars by 8.90; DB 11 Squadron Dhahran by 16–17.9.90; modified to S1+; B BFME DD 11 Squadron Leeming by 7.91.

ZE205T     F/f 18.9.86; AJ 229 OCU 16.10.86; ASF Coningsby 29.1.87; AA 229 OCU Coningsby 6.87; BF 29 Squadron 5C Squadron Dhahran 10.8.90; AA 229 OCU Coningsby; 56R Squadron Coningsby by 10.92.

ZE206     F/f 5.11.86; ASF 28.4.87; BF 29 Squadron Coningsby 5.87; GG 43 Squadron Leuchars; DC 11 Squadron Dhahran 29–30.8.90; modified to S1+; C BFME EW 23 Squadron Leeming by 5.91; borrowed by Leuchars wing for Distant Frontier 92, 4.92. FH25 Squadron Leeming by 10.94.

ZE207     F/f 7.9.87; BAe; ASF 23.10.87; BL 29 Squadron 1.88; BBF as BJ 29 Squadron; CK 5 Squadron Coningsby by 4.91; GC 43 Squadron Leuchars by 8.91.

ZE208T     F/f 27.11.86; ASF 16.12.86; BT 29 Squadron Coningsby 3.87; DZ St Athan by 8.91 used for MLO trials; 56R Squadron Coningsby by 10.92; AN 229 OCU 56R Squadron Coningsby by 1.93.

ZE209    F/f 26.1.87; BC 29 Squadron Coningsby 6.2.87; first of unit noted 3.87; AS 229 OCU Coningsby; BBF AS 229 OCU 65R Squadron; 1435 Flight Falklands 8.7.92. AV 56R Squadron by 9.94.

ZE210    F/f 27.1.87; ASF 11.2.87; OEU Coningsby 7.87; GL 43 Squadron Leuchars by 8.90; DD 11 Squadron Dhahran on 29–30.8.90; modified to S1+; G 11 Squadron Leeming by 1.91; 43 Squadron Leuchars on 14.3.91; G 25 Squadron Leeming by 5.91; FB 25 Squadron Leeming; borrowed by Leuchars wing 4.92 for Distant Frontier 92.

ZE250    F/f 29.1.87; ASF 24.2.87; AP 229 OCU Coningsby 7.87; loaned to 29 Squadron 8.87; AF 229 OCU Coningsby 1.88; EQ 23 Squadron Leeming; HZ 111 Squadron Leuchars; suffered engine fire as HZ 111 Squadron Leuchars early 1992; HZ stored RAF Leuchars; still in aircraft servicing hangar at Leuchars 18.9.93; Leuchars on repair 1.94.

ZE251    F/f 13.2.87; ASF 24.2.87; OEU 7.87; F3 OEU; 11 Squadron Leeming by 1.91; DE 11 Squadron Leeming; DE stored St Athan by 7.93.

ZE252    F/f 4.3.87; ASF 28.4.87; OEU 7.87; AY 229 OCU Coningsby; F3 OEU; HH 111 Squadron Leuchars by 12.91.

ZE253T    F/f 9.3.87; delivered 25.3.87; retained by BAe; AB 229 OCU Coningsby 12.87; AB 229 OCU Coningsby 1990; BBF as AB 65R Squadron; AC 56R Squadron Coningsby by 10.92.

ZE254    F/f 12.3.87; ASF 20.3.87; BG 29 Squadron Coningsby 4.87; BG 29 Squadron; 5C Squadron Dhahran

10.8.90; CA 5 Squadron Coningsby by 4.91; CA 5 Squadron Coningsby by 8.91; stored St Athan by 7.93.

ZE255 F/f 24.3.87; BH 29 Squadron 2.4.87; first 29 Squadron aircraft to fly 29.4.87; BH 29 Squadron 5C Squadron Dhahran 10.8.90; BH 111 Squadron Leuchars by 7.91; HI 111 Squadron Leuchars by 12.91; HI stored St Athan by 7.93.

ZE256T F/f 31.3.87; ASF 8.4.87; painted in trial 5 Squadron markings 6.87; 29 Squadron Coningsby 8.87; CT 5 Squadron 11.87; BBF as AJ 65R Squadron; AJ 56R Squadron Coningsby by 10.92.

ZE257 F/f 14.4.87; BD 29 Squadron 28.4.87; BD 29 Squadron Coningsby; BBF as BD 29 Squadron 1992; HN 111 Squadron Leuchars by 4.93.

ZE258 F/f 21.5.87; BE 29 Squadron Coningsby 12.6.87; CT 5 Squadron Coningsby; BE 29 Squadron; BE 5 Composite Squadron Dhahran 10.8.90; CJ 5 Squadron Coningsby by 4.91; GA 43 Squadron Leuchars by 7.91; GA RAF Coningsby by 3.93; GA stored St Athan by 7.93.

ZE287 F/f 1.5.87; AE 229 OCU Coningsby 21.5.87; AH 56R Squadron Coningsby by 12.92.

ZE288 F/f 5.6.87; BI 29 Squadron Coningsby 25.6.87; BI 29 Squadron Coningsby; 43 Squadron Leuchars by 5.91; GG stored at St Athan by 7.93.

ZE289 F/f 12.6.87; BJ 29 Squadron Coningsby 13.8.87; BA 29 Squadron Coningsby 1990; BA 29 Squadron 5C Squadron Dhahran 10.8.90; HK HF 111 Squadron Leuchars by 12.91, nosewheel collapsed on landing at Leuchars in 7.92; ASF Leuchars by 3.92; flying again as HF 111 Squadron Leuchars by 6.94.

ZE290    F/f 9.7.87; AD 229 OCU Coningsby 2.10.87; FE 25 Squadron Leeming; BBF 25 Squadron; AT 229 OCU Coningsby by 5.91; AD 56R Squadron Coningsby by 12.92.

ZE291    F/f 30.7.87; BK 29 Squadron Coningsby 18.9.87; BBF as AZ 65R Squadron; AZ 56R Squadron Coningsby by 10.92; 43 Squadron still coded AZ Leuchars by 1.93; AZ ASF Leuchars 12.93. GQ 43 Squadron Leuchars by 4.94.

ZE292    F/f 6.8.87; ASF 25.9.87; CA 5 Squadron Coningsby 11.87; first aircraft for 5 Squadron 25.9.87; AU 229 OCU Coningsby 1992; AU 56R Squadron Coningsby by 10.92; HA 111 Squadron Leuchars by 4.93; this aircraft was damaged at RAF St Athan during airframe modification by a private contractor in May 1993; after return to Squadron was returned to St Athan for storage awaiting repair.

ZE293    F/f 26.8.87; AC 229 OCU Coningsby 9.10.87; AC 229 OCU Coningsby 1992; HT 111 Squadron Leuchars by 4.93.

ZE294    ASF 19.10.87; CB 5 Squadron Coningsby 1.88; AQ 229 OCU Coningsby 1992; AQ 56R Squadron Coningsby by 10.92; AQ stored at St Athan by 7.93.

ZE295    CC 5 Squadron Coningsby 19.10.87;; AR 229 OCU Coningsby 1992; AR 56R Squadron Coningsby by 10.92; AW 56R Squadron by 5.93; was damaged by private contractor at St Athan during airframe mods May 1993; after rejoining unit was returned to St Athan for storage awaiting repair; stored RAF Coningsby.

ZE296T  AM 229 OCU Coningsby 19.10.87; AM 229 OCU 1992; AM 56R Squadron Coningsby by 10.92; AM 43 Squadron Leuchars by 3.93; GR 43 Squadron Leuchars by 12.93.

ZE338  ASF 26.10.87; CD 5 Squadron 1.88; BB 29 Squadron 5C Squadron Dhahran 10.8.90; BBF as BB 29 Squadron; BB 111 Squadron Leuchars 1992; HG 111 Squadron Leuchars.

ZE339  CE 5 Squadron Coningsby 26.10.87; AX 229 OCU Coningsby; FO 25 Squadron Leeming by 4.93; FO 29 Squadron Coningsby by 7.93; FQ 25 Squadron Leeming by 4.94.

ZE340T  ASF 30.10.87; AG 229 OCU Coningsby 12.87; AG 229 OCU Coningsby 1990; BBF as AG 65R Squadron; AE 56R Squadron Coningsby by 10.92.

ZE341  ASF 6.11.87; CF 5 Squadron Coningsby 1.88; HD 111 Squadron Leuchars by 12.91.

ZE342  ASF 20.11.87; CG 5 Squadron 1.88; BBF as BK 29 Squadron; HE 111 Squadron Leuchars by 12.91; BL 29 Squadron Coningsby by 1.93; HW 111 Squadron Leuchars by 10.94.

ZE343T  ASF 20.11,87; AN 229 OCU Coningsby 1.88; AI 229 OCU Coningsby 1992; AI 56R Squadron Coningsby by 10.92; damaged by a private contractor during airframe modifications May 1993; after return to unit was sent back to St Athan for storage awaiting repair; stored RAF Coningsby; to St Athan for storage by 12.93.

ZE728T  A&AEE Bascombe Down 22.10.87; BBF as BF 29 Squadron; AN 229 OCU Coningsby 1992; AN 56R Squadron Coningsby by 10.92; AL 56R Squadron

Coningsby by 5.93; damaged at St Athan by private contractor during airframe mods; after rejoining unit was returned to St Athan for storage awaiting repair; stored RAF Coningsby; stored St Athan.

ZE729T    OEU 21.12.87; EC 23 Squadron Leeming; F3 OEU Coningsby; BF 29 Squadron Coningsby by 7.91; BF stored St Athan by 7.93.

ZE730    OEU 21.12.87; BBF as DF 11 Squadron; CD 5 Squadron Coningsby by 4.91; GL 43 Squadron Leuchars by 12.91; GL 43 Squadron Leuchars by 7.93.

ZE731    OEU 21.12.87; F3 OEU Coningsby; CH 5 Squadron Coningsby by 4.91; 111 Squadron Leuchars by 5.91; GK 43 Squadron Leuchars by 12.91.

ZE732    CH 5 Squadron Coningsby 1.88; CH 5C Squadron Dhahran 8.90; GI 43 Squadron Leuchars by 12.91.

ZE733    CI 5 Squadron Coningsby 1.88; FH 25 Squadron Leeming; BBF as FH 25 Squadron; CL 5 Squadron Coningsby by 4.91; GE 43 Squadron Leuchars 1992.

ZE734    CJ 5 Squadron Coningsby 1.88; took part in ADEX 90–2, 3.90; CJ 5C Squadron Dhahran 8.90; CJ 5 Squadron Coningsby by 5.91; CX 5 Squadron Coningsby by 5.92; GE 43 Squadron Leuchars; GB 43 Squadron Leuchars by 4.94.

ZE735T    CT 5 Squadron Coningsby; FE 25 Squadron Leeming; BBF as FE 25 Squadron; AL 229 OCU Coningsby 1992; AL 56R Squadron Coningsby by 10.92; AL stored RAF Coningsby; AL ASF Coningsby by 4.94.

ZE736    CK 5 Squadron Coningsby; CK 5 C Squadron Dhahran 8.90; HA 111 Squadron Leuchars by 7.91; stored St Athan by 7.93.

ZE737　CE 5 Squadron Coningsby; took part in ADEX 90–2, 3.90; 11 Squadron Leeming by 1.91; K 43 Squadron on 14.3.91; FF 25 Squadron Leeming by 7.91.

ZE755　GB 43 Squadron Leuchars by 7.91.

ZE756　BAe Warton 1992; F3 OEU Coningsby 1993.

ZE757　GF 43 Squadron Leuchars by 7.91; GF stored RAF St Athan; GA 43 Squadron Leuchars by 12.93. GF 43 Squadron Leuchars by 10.94.

ZE758　CB 5 Squadron Coningsby; CB 5C Squadron Dhahran 8.90; BH 29 Squadron Coningsby by 7.91; C 1435 flight FI. HV111 Squadron Leuchars by 10.94.

ZE759T　FC 25 Squadron Leeming; BT 29 Squadron Coningsby; A3 229 OCU Coningsby by 12.91; AG 56R Squadron Coningsby by 10.92; AG stored St Athan by 7.93.

ZE760　CF 5 Squadron Coningsby; BBF as CF 5 Squadron; AP 229 OCU Coningsby; made a successful belly landing at Coningsby as AP 229 OCU on 6.6.90; was flying again by August still coded AP, received unofficial tail art; BY 29 Squadron Coningsby by 10.91; P 43 Squadron Leuchars 1993.

ZE761　First aircraft to arrive at Leeming 28.3.88; BBF as CC 5 Squadron; CB 5 Squadron Coningsby by 7.91.

ZE762　CA 5 Squadron Coningsby; took part in ADEX 90–2,3.90; CH 5C Squadron Dhahran 8.90; CD 5 Squadron Coningsby by 8.91; AX 229 OCU Coningsby 1992; BB 29 Squadron Coningsby by 5.92; 43 Squadron Leuchars by 5.93; coded GM 43 Squadron Leuchars.

ZE763　CD 5 Squadron Coningsby; A 11 Squadron Leeming by 1.91; CD 5 Squadron Coningsby by 5.91; BA 29

Squadron Coningsby by 8.91; BA 23 Squadron Leeming 1992; took part in first Red Flag exercise by Tornado F3 1.93; BA 11 Squadron Leeming by 4.93; DG 11 Squadron Leeming by 7.93.

ZE764    First aircraft for 11 Squadron arrived 25.4.88 coded DH was C/Os aircraft specially painted with black tailfin and spine; HC 111 Squadron Leuchars by 11.90; BFME 43C Squadron Dhahran upgraded to S1+; I 43 Squadron Leuchars on 14.3.91; DH 11 Squadron Leeming 1992.

ZE785    DA 11 Squadron Leeming; BBF as DA 11 Squadron; AO 229 OCU (65R) Squadron received special anniversary markings for 65R Squadron 75th anniversary 1990; AO 56R Squadron Coningsby by 10.92; stored St Athan by 7.93; AT 56R Squadron Coningsby by 5.94.

ZE786T    DT 11 Squadron Leeming; CF 5 Squadron Coningsby by 8.91; CT 5 Squadron Coningsby by 12.91; CT stored St Athan by 7.93.

ZE787    DB 11 Squadron Leeming 1990; AV 229 OCU Coningsby; EX 23 Squadron Leeming by 10.92.

ZE788    DC 11 Squadron Leeming; S 11 Squadron Leeming by 1.91; FH 25 Squadron Leeming by 7.91; DF 11 Squadron Leeming by 4.93.

ZE789    DD 11 Squadron Leeming; FI 25 Squadron Leeming by 8.90; BBF DD 11 Squadron; 43 Squadron Leuchars by 5.91; FI 25 Squadron Leeming by 7.91; AW 229 OCU Coningsby by 8.91; AW 56R Squadron Coningsby by 10.92; AW stored St Athan by 7.93; AU 56R Squadron Coningsby by 6.94.

ZE790    HC 111 Squadron Leuchars by 12.91; as HC flew in formation with all black Hunters to commemorate the Black Arrows; D 1435 Flight RAF Mount Pleasant Falkland Islands by 11.92; 56R Squadron Coningsby by 5.94; AW 56R Squadron Coningsby by 7.94.

ZE791T    BBF as FF 25 Squadron; A9 229 OCU Coningsby by 10.91; A9 56R Squadron Coningsby by 10.92.

ZE792    DG 11 Squadron Leeming; CE 5 Squadron Coningsby by 4.91; 43 Squadron Leuchars by 5.91; GJ 43 Squadron Leuchars by 12.91; GJ 43 Squadron Leuchars 1992; 1435 Flight Falklands 8.7.92; CU 5 Squadron Coningsby; HL 111 Squadron Leuchars by 4.93.

ZE793T    DZ 11 Squadron Coningsby; BBF as DZ 11 Squadron; AK 229 OCU Coningsby; AK 56R Squadron Coningsby by 10.92; AK stored St Athan by 7.93.

ZE794T    11 Squadron Leeming; FD 25 Squadron Leeming; 43 Squadron Leuchars by 1.91; A4 229 OCU Coningsby by 10.91; HQ 111 Squadron Leuchars by 6.92; A4 111 Squadron Leuchars by 7.93; HQ 111 Squadron Leuchars by 12.93.

ZE808    DJ 11 Squadron Leeming; BBF as DJ 11 Squadron; GF 43 Squadron Leuchars by 11.90; C 11 Squadron Leeming by 4.91; FA 25 Squadron Leeming by 7.91; was used as reserve display aircraft for the 1991 season; borrowed by Leuchars wing 4.92 for Distant Frontier 92; received new tail markings of 25 in Roman Numerals along with repositioned code letters by 9.94.

ZE809    First aircraft for 23 Squadron arrived 5.8.88; this aircraft was specially painted with a red and blue fin with a red eagle in a white circle for the unit's 75th anniversary in 1990; EZ 23 Squadron Leeming; BBF as EZ 23 Squadron; CE 5 Squadron Coningsby by 8.91; HP 111 Squadron Leuchars; as loaned to 11 Squadron Leeming by 3.94 until W/O when it crashed into the North Sea 60 miles N E of Newcastle 7.6.94.

ZE810T    EN 23 Squadron Leeming; EN 23 Squadron Leeming by 7.91; upgraded to S1+; A8 229 OCU Coningsby by 10.91; FB 25 Squadron Leeming, detached to Goose Bay Canada 1992; 56R Squadron Coningsby by 10.92; AT 56R Squadron Coningsby by 7.93.

ZE811    DI 11 Squadron Leeming; BBF as DI 11 Squadron; HB 111 Squadron Leuchars.

ZE812T    EA 23 Squadron Leeming 1990; BBF as EA 23 Squadron; AY 229 OCU Coningsby by 10.91; F 1435 Flight RAF Mount Pleasant Falkland Islands by 10.92; 56R Squadron Coningsby by 9.94.

ZE830    ET 23 Squadron Leeming; BBF as ET 23 Squadron; GD 43 Squadron Leuchars by 7.91.

ZE831    EW 23 Squadron Leeming; BBF as EW 23 Squadron; 43 Squadron Leuchars by 5.91; HJ 111 Squadron Leuchars 1992; GG 43 Squadron Leuchars by 12.93.

ZE832T    EB 23 Squadron Leeming; 43 Squadron Leuchars by 5.91; A7 229 OCU Coningsby by 10.91; A7 56R Squadron Coningsby by 10.92.

ZE833    EC 23 Squadron Leeming; W/O as EC 23 Squadron when crashed into North Sea 35nm NE of Newcastle 21.7.89.

ZE834    ED 23 Squadron Leeming; RAF Leeming on repair.

ZE835    EE 23 Squadron Leeming; EE 111 Squadron Leuchars by 12.91; HK 111 Squadron Leuchars.

ZE836    EF 23 Squadron Leeming; BBF as EF 23 Squadron; CH 5 Squadron Coningsby by 8.91; CH 25 Squadron Leeming 1992; AS 56R Squadron Coningsby by 10.92.

ZE837    EQ 23 Squadron Leeming; FL 25 Squadron Leeming by 8.90; BBF as EA 25 Squadron; CF 5 Squadron Coningsby by 4.91; DJ 11 Squadron Leeming 1992; HY 111 Squadron Leuchars.

ZE838    FA 25 Squadron Leeming; BBF as FA 25 Squadron; specially painted for 75th anniversary, normal fin with large white middle centre section with white upper fuselage, 1915—1990 on fin with unit badge; BB 29 Squadron Coningsby 1992; GH 43 Squadron Leuchars.

ZE839T    EG 23 Squadron Leeming; A6 229 OCU Coningsby by 10.91; A6 56R Squadron Coningsby by 10.92; AR 56R Squadron Coningsby by 7.93; this aircraft was the 1993 solo display ship.

ZE858T    First aircraft for 25 Squadron coded FK, arrived Leeming 15.12.88 wearing a large ? on the tail fin as third Leeming Squadron had not yet been chosen; FB 25 Squadron Leeming; BBF as FB 25 Squadron; A5 229 OCU Coningsby by 10.91; A5 43 Squadron Leuchars; GO 43 Squadron Leuchars by August 93; W/O after crashing in Cumbria as Go 43 Squadron 21.10.93.

ZE862T    J F3 OEU Coningsby; by 1992.

ZE887    GE 43 Squadron Leuchars; DE 11 Squadron Leeming 10.90; modified to S1+ for Gulf ops but retained at Leeming; E BFME DJ 11 Squadron Leeming by 7.91; took part in Red Flag 93–1, 1.93.

ZE888    F3 OEU Coningsby; DT 11 Squadron Dhahran on 16–17.9.90; modified to S1+; T 11 Squadron Leeming by 1.91; EV 23 Squadron Leeming by 7.91; EV 25 Squadron Leeming by 6.94. EV 43 Squadron Leuchars by 9.94.

ZE889    F3 OEU Coningsby by 1992; Received special OEU markings of a red chevron with the letters AWC in a white circle, the AWC is the Air Warfare Centre, the aircraft was given unusual SB tailcode as these are the initials of the OEU boss Stu Black; deployed to Mountain Home AFB USA August 1994 for JTIDS trials.

ZE907    Was painted with red white striped fin and red upper fuselage for 1990 display season, had special Battle of Britain 50th anniversary markings on forward fuselage; DK 11 Squadron Dhahran 21–22.9.90; K BFME; EN 23 Squadron Leeming 1992; EN 43 Squadron Leuchars by 9.94.

ZE908    CT 5 Squadron Coningsby; modified to S1+ for Gulf ops, deployed to Dhahran 11.90 uncoded; X BFME 43 Squadron Leuchars by 1.91; BFME; FC 25 Squadron Leeming 1992.

ZE911    BE 29 Squadron Coningsby by 12.91.

ZE934T   GH 43 Squadron Leuchars; DG 11 Squadron Dhahran on 16–17.9.90; modified to S1+ Q BFME Dhahran; CE 5 Squadron Coningsby; DX 11 Squadron Leeming by 5.91.

ZE936    GK 43 Squadron Leuchars 1990; 25 Squadron Leeming; DF 11 Squadron Dhahran on 29–30.8.90; F BFME F 11 Squadron Leeming by 1.91; EE 23 Squadron Leeming by 7.91; borrowed by Leuchars wing

4.92 for Distant Frontier 92; DL 11 Squadron Leeming
by 9.94.

ZE941T    GH 43 Squadron Leuchars 1989; CI 5 Squadron
Coningsby; DW 11 Squadron Dhahran on 21–
22.9.90; modified to S1+; DY 11 Squadron Leeming
by 7.91; FE 25 Squadron Leeming by 5.93.

ZE942    DK 11 Squadron Leeming by 7.91.

ZE961    Together with 962 was first aircraft for 43 Squadron
on 23.9.89 coded GA; DH 11 Squadron Dhahran on
29–30.8.90; modified to S1+; H BFME FD 25 Squadron Leeming by 8.91; borrowed by Leuchars wing for
Distant Frontier 92.

ZE962    Together with 961 was first 43 Squadron aircraft
arrived on 23.9.89 coded GB; DI 11 Squadron Dhahran on 29–30.8.90; modified to S1+; I 11 Squadron
Leeming by 1.91; FJ 11 Squadron Leeming; FG 25
Squadron Leeming.

ZE963    First aircraft for Leuchars wing arrived from Warton
23.8.89; coded GC for 43 Squadron; DX 11 Squadron
Dhahran 21–22.9.90; modified to S1+; ET 23 Squadron Leeming 1992; ET 25 Squadron Leeming by 7.94;
FT 25 Squadron Leeming by 10.94.

ZE964    Leuchars wing; DS 11 Squadron Leeming August
1990, modified to S1+ for Gulf ops but remained at
Leeming; J 43 Squadron Leuchars on 14.3.91; EU 23
Squadron Leeming by 5.91; DY 11 Squadron Leeming
by 5.93.

ZE965    HA 111 Squadron Leuchars; DY 11 Squadron Leeming August 1990 modified to S1+ for Gulf operations
but retained at Leeming; BZ 29 Squadron Coningsby
1992; DW 11 Squadron Leeming by 7.93.

ZE966    DZ 11 Squadron Leeming; GF 43 Squadron Leuchars on 14.3.91; DZ 11 Squadron Leeming.

ZE967    Leuchars wing; DR 11 Squadron Leeming by 9.90; modified to S1+ for operations in the Gulf but did not deploy, remained at Leeming; 43 Squadron Leuchars on 14.3.91; FE 25 Squadron Leeming by 5.91; EU 23 Squadron Leeming by 4.93; FU 25 Squadron Leeming by 7.94.

ZE968    HE 111 Squadron Leuchars by 8.90; DJ 11 Squadron Dhahran on 29–30.8.90 received Desert Eagle badge on fin; J BFME BA 29 Squadron Coningsby by 12.91; BA 29 Squadron Coningsby; F3 OEU Coningsby by 1992.

ZE969    HD 111 Squadron Leuchars by 8.90; DL 11 Squadron on 16–17.8.90; L 11 Squadron Leeming by 5.91; EA 23 Squadron Leeming 1992; DI 11 Squadron Leeming by 9.94.

ZE982    BAe Warton; DP 11 Squadron Dhahran 16–17.9.90; P DM 11 Squadron Leeming 1992; took part in first Red Flag for F3 93-1, 1.93.

ZE983    B 11 Squadron Leeming by 1.91; upgraded to S1+; BFME Dhahran; 43 Squadron Leuchars on 14.3.91; EZ 23 Squadron Leeming by 5.91; HP 111 Squadron Gio del Colle Italy; by 8.94 this aircraft had not been based at Leuchars with 111 Squadron.

ZG728    229 OCU Coningsby by 8.90; CI 5 Squadron Coningsby by 4.91.

ZG730    CC 5 Squadron Coningsby by 4.91.

ZG731    CG 5 Squadron Coningsby by 4.91.

ZG732    BC 29 Squadron Coningsby by 8.91.

ZG733    BK 29 Squadron Coningsby by 8.91.

ZG734      CJ 5 Squadron Coningsby by 10.91; BG 29 Squadron
           Coningsby.

ZG735      CO 5 Squadron Coningsby by 10.91.

ZG751      CW 5 Squadron Coningsby by 12.91; CW ASF Con-
           ingsby by 4.94.

ZG753      CH 5 Squadron Coningsby.

ZG755      GM 43 Squadron Leuchars by 12.91; 43 Squadron
           Leuchars by 3.93; 5 Squadron Coningsby by 4.93; BB
           29 Squadron Coningsby by 5.93.

ZG757      HL 111 Squadron Leuchars by 12.91; CA 5 Squadron
           Coningsby by 3.93; CA 56R Squadron Coningsby by
           6.94.

ZG768      56R Squadron Coningsby by 10.92; AX 56R Squad-
           ron Coningsby by 12.92.

ZG770      AP 56R Squadron Coningsby by 10.92. BD 29 Squad-
           ron Coningsby by 10.94.

ZG772      CN 5 Squadron Coningsby.

ZG774      GN 43 Squadron Leuchars. AY 56R Squadron Con-
           ingsby by 10.94.

ZG776      HN 111 Squadron Leuchars by 3.93; BD 29 Squadron
           Coningsby by 5.93; 56R Squadron Coningsby by
           6.94.

ZG778      111 Squadron Leuchars by 3.93; HC 111 Squadron
           Leuchars by 4.93. 25 Squadron Leeming by 9.94.

ZG780      BH 29 Squadron Coningsby by 9.92.

ZG793      56R Squadron Coningsby by 10.92; CY 5 Squadron
           Coningsby by 3.93.

ZG795      AY 56R Squadron Coningsby by 10.92. CB 5 Squad-
           ron Coningsby by 9.94.

ZG796      AV 56R Squadron Coningsby.

ZG797 AU 56R Squadron Coningsby; BF 29 Squadron Coningsby by 4.94.

ZG798 CS 5 Squadron Coningsby by 1.93.

ZG799 AQ 56R Squadron Coningsby by 1.93.

ZH552 Delivered to Coningsby on 11.9.92, coded AZ 56R Squadron by 12.92; F3 OEU Coningsby by 10.94.

ZH553 BY 29 Squadron Coningsby by 3.93.

ZH554 GJ 43 Squadron Leuchars by 3.93; 29 Squadron Coningsby by 4.94. BZ 29 Squadron Coningsby by 10.94.

ZH555 CV 5 Squadron Coningsby by 5.93.

ZH556 AK 56R Squadron Coningsby by 3.93.

ZH557 AB 56R Squadron Coningsby by 5.93. CT 5 Squadron Coningsby by 9.94.

ZH558 GF 43 Squadron Leuchars by 4.93; WO as GF 43 Squadron 8.7.94, crashed into Mediterranean Sea off Cyprus while based at Akratori on extended 7 week APC.

ZH559 Handed over to RAF as last F3 on 24.3.93 RAF Coningsby; AO 56R Squadron Coningsby by 5.93.

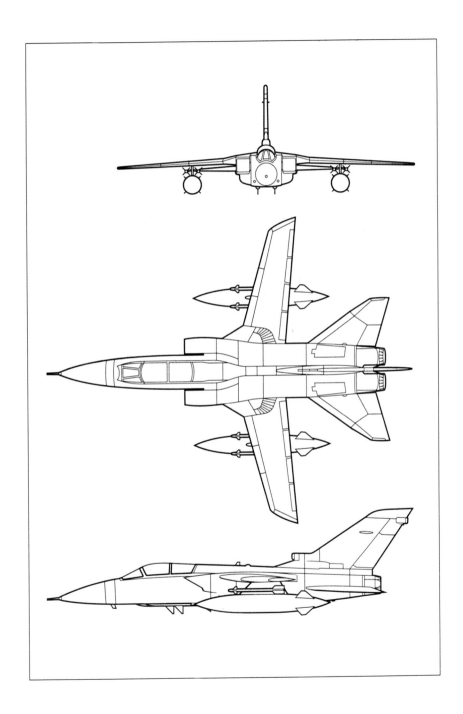

# Late Information

## Individual Aircraft Histories

ZD901    AA BAe Warton by road, 24.10.94

ZD902    MOD (PE) Bascombe Down by 11.94

ZE154    AD BAe Warton by road, 24.1.94

ZE161    FG 25 Squadron Leeming by 12.94

ZE201    DO 11 Squadron Leeming by 11.94

ZE205    DT 11 Squadron Leeming

ZE257    FZ 25 Squadron Leeming by 11.94

ZE291    GQ 25 Squadron Leuchars deployed by Nellis AFB USA for Red Flag 95–1 1–12.10.94 then returned to Leuchars

ZE339    AQ 56R Squadron Coningsby, 1.95

ZE 732   AS 56R Squadron Coningsby by 1.95

ZE733    GE 43 Squadron Leuchars deployed to Nellis AFB USA for Red Flag 95–1 1–12.10.94 then returned to Leuchars

ZE789    Was W/O as AU 56R Squadron when it crashed into North Sea, 10.3.95

ZE791    FP 25 Squadron Leeming by 1.95

ZE907    FM 25 Squadron Leeming by 11.94

ZG753    1435 Flt Falkland Islands

| ZG755 | 1435 Flt Falkland Islands |
| ZG757 | CA 5 Squadron Falkland Islands |
| ZG776 | 1435 Flt Falkland Islands |
| ZG778 | 25 Squadron Leeming by 1.95 |
| ZG799 | BB 29 Squadron Coningsby |

During late 1994 BAe started repair work on the first of the more seriously damaged of the 18 aircraft damaged by Airwork in 1993, three less seriously damaged aircraft having already been repaired and returned to service. BAe was given a contract for a trial rebuild of Tornado F3 ZE154 using the centre section of Tornado F2 ZD901. Both these aircraft were in storage at St Athan from where they were taken by road to BAe Warton on 24 October 1994. Of the 18 F2s built (excluding the three prototypes) ZD899 and ZD939 are serving with the MOD (PE) BAe Warton, ZD900 is with the A&AEE Bascombe Down and ZD 902 is with the DRA also at Bascombe Down. This leaves the other 14 aircraft, 13 of which are stored at St Athan and the other at Coningsby. ZD901, ZD903–ZD906, ZD932–ZD938 and ZD940–ZD941 are available for use in the rebuild programme if the trial is successful. Other F3s in storage at St Athan awaiting a decision on the rebuild programme are ZE251, ZE254, ZE258, ZE288, ZE292, ZE294, ZE295, ZE343, ZE728, ZE729, ZE736, ZE759, ZE786 and ZE793.

In November 1994 11 Squadron Leeming took over the Deny Flight detachment at Gio del Colle for the second time, restarting the cycle of F3 units. 25 Squadron also Leeming took over in February 1995, also for the second time.

The RAF lost another Tornado F3 ZE789 AU 56R Squadron when it crashed into the North Sea 5 miles (8km) off Spurn Point on 10 March 1995. Both crew members ejected and were picked up by helicopter although the navigator was killed.

RAF Tornado F3s patrolling the skies over Bosnia are expected to receive the GEC Marconi Ariel towed radar decoy during 1995 for added protection against SAM threats.

# Glossary

| | |
|---|---|
| A&AEE | Aircraft and Armament Experimental Establishment. |
| AAA | Anti Aircraft Artillery. |
| AAM | Air to Air Missile. |
| ACMI | Air Combat Manoeuvring Instrumentation. |
| AD | Air Defence. |
| ADEX | Air Defence Exercise. |
| ADV | Air Defence Variant. |
| AEW | Airborne Early Warning. |
| AEZ | Air Exclusion Zone. |
| AI | Airborne Interception |
| AIM | Airborne Interception Missile. |
| AIREX | Air Exercise. |
| ALARM | Air Launched Anti Radiation Missile. |
| AMRAAM | Advanced Medium Range Air to Air Missile. |
| APC | Armament Practice Camp. |
| ASF | Aircraft Serving Flight. |
| ASM | Anti Ship Missile. |
| ASRAAM | Advanced Short Range Air to Air Missile. |
| ATC | Air Traffic Control. |
| AWACS | Airborne Warning and Control System. |
| BA | British Airways. |
| BAC | British Aircraft Corporation. |
| BAe | British Aerospace. |

| | |
|---|---|
| BBF | Battle of Britain Fly Past. |
| BBMF | Battle of Britain Memorial Flight. |
| BDRT | Battle Damage Repair Training. |
| BFME | British Forces Middle East. |
| BVR | Beyond Visual Range. |
| CAA | Civil Aviation Authority. |
| CAP | Combat Air Patrol. |
| CFS | Central Flying School. |
| CIS | Commonwealth of Independent States. |
| CO | Commanding Officer. |
| CONVEX | Conversion Exercise. |
| CRT | Cathode Ray Tube. |
| DACT | Dissimilar Air Combat Training. |
| DECU | Digital Engine Control Unit. |
| DRA | Defence Research Agency. |
| ECCM | Electronic Counter Counter Measures. |
| ECM | Electronic Counter Measures. |
| ECR | Electronic Combat Reconnaissance. |
| EFA | European Fighter Aircraft. |
| F | Fighter. |
| FA | Fighter Attack. |
| FGR | Fighter Ground Attack Reconnaissance. |
| FI | Falkland Islands. |
| FLIR | Forward Looking Infra Red. |
| FMICW | Frequency Modulated Interrupted Continuous Wave. |
| FTS | Flying Training School. |
| GCI | Ground Controlled Intercept. |
| GR | Ground Attack Recce. |
| HARM | High Speed Anti Radiation Missile. |
| HAS | Hardened Aircraft Shelter. |
| HMS | Her Majesty's Ship. |

| | |
|---|---|
| HOTAS | Hands on Throttle and Stick. |
| HQ | Head Quarters. |
| HUD | Head Up Display. |
| IDS | Interdictor Strike. |
| IMN | Indicated Mach Number. |
| INS | Inertial Navigation System. |
| IRST | Infra Red Search and Track. |
| JASDF | Japanese Air Self Defence Force. |
| JTIDS | Joint Tactical Information Distribution System. |
| K | Tanker. |
| IAS | Indicated Air Speed. |
| MDC | Miniature Detonating Cord. |
| MFF | Mixed Fighter Force. |
| MLO | Mid Life Overhaul. |
| Mod | Ministry Of Defence. |
| MOD (PE) | Ministry Of Defence Procurement Executive. |
| MOU | Memorandum of Understanding. |
| MPC | Missile Practice Camp. |
| MR | Maritime Reconnaissance. |
| MRCA | Multi Role Combat Aircraft. |
| MU | Maintenance Unit. |
| NAS | Naval Air Squadron. |
| NATO | North Atlantic Treaty Organisation. |
| NVG | Night Vision Goggles. |
| OC | Officer Commanding. |
| OCU | Operational Conversion Unit. |
| OEU | Operation Evaluation Unit. |
| PRF | Pulse Repetition Frequency. |
| QRA | Quick Reaction Alert. |
| RAAF | Royal Australian Air Force. |
| RAE | Royal Aircraft Establishment. |

| | |
|---|---|
| RAF | Royal Air Force. |
| RAM | Radar Absorbent Material. |
| RCS | Radar Cross Section. |
| RFA | Royal Fleet Auxiliary. |
| RHWR | Radar Homing and Warning Receiver. |
| RMAF | Royal Malaysian Air Force. |
| RN | Royal Navy. |
| RSAF | Royal Saudi Air Force. |
| RWR | Radar Warning Receiver. |
| SACLANT | Supreme Allied Commander Atlantic. |
| SACUER | Supreme Allied Commander Europe. |
| SAM | Surface to Air Missile. |
| SARH | Semi Active Radar Homing. |
| SOC | Sector Operations Centre. |
| Sqn | Squadron. |
| SST | Supersonic Transport. |
| STCAAME | Strike Command Air to Air Missile Establishment. |
| TASF | Tornado Aircraft Servicing Flight. |
| TPF | Tornado Propulsion Flight. |
| TV | Television. |
| TWCU | Tactical Weapons Conversion Unit. |
| TWU | Tactical Weapons Unit. |
| UK | United Kingdom. |
| UKADR | United Kingdom Air Defence Region. |
| UN | United Nations. |
| USAF | United States Air Force. |
| USAFE | United States Air Force Europe. |
| USS | United States Ship. |
| WO | Written Off. |